THE
Bay Area
at
YOUR
FEET

Previous books by Margot Patterson Doss
San Francisco At Your Feet
Golden Gate Park At Your Feet
Walks for Children in San Francisco

"I saw a multitude of men coming toward us — I saw them coming from every direction, filling all the roads."

St. Francis of Assisi

Dedication

It is to this advancing multitude that I dedicate this book of loving exploration. May they treasure and protect the sweet land that is the Bay Area. Now, Before it is too late.

THE
BAY
AREA
at
YOUR
FEET

By Margot Patterson Doss
with photos by John Whinham Doss, M.D.

Chronicle Books
SAN FRANCISCO

Introduction

▪ The pleasures of walking, particularly of walking in the Bay Area, were what I planned to consider in this introduction. Ours is a more pleasurable place to walk than most metropolitan places. However, it gets less so every day. So this is my subject instead, which by extension becomes man's place in nature.

In pursuing it, I went back to read what other walkers had written in their time. One beautiful passage by George Macaulay Trevelyan in his essay *Walking* embodies the kernel of the problem in a gentle prophecy.

"From out of the depth of days and nights gone by and forgotten, I have a vision not forgettable, of making the steep ascent to Volterra (read Mount Tamalpais if you will) for the first time, under the circlings of the stars, the smell of unseen almond blossom in the air; the lights of Italy far below us; ancient Tuscany just above us, where we were to sup and sleep guarded by the giant walls. Few went to Volterra then, but years have passed, and now I am glad to think that many go, *faute de mieux*, in motor cars; yet so they cannot hear the silence we heard, or smell the almond blossom we smelt, and if they did, they could not feel them as the walker can feel."

If Trevelyan were to write his essay today, I think he would no longer be glad to think that many go to Volterra in motor cars. I am not glad that motor cars go up Mount Tam. For the motor car has been revealed as a Frankenstein in our culture, destroying not only the silence and the smell of almond blossom, but the air, the land, and the oceans too in its hunger for fossil fuels. Indeed the pleasures that the automobile seemed to make accessible to all, the almond orchards and the vast starry silent places, have been among its victims. Today the best favor one can do anyplace is to leave it inaccessible. Not to build a road to it.

Not long ago a member of the East Bay Regional Park district arranged for me to visit Brooks Island for a walk around it. It was an enlightening experience.

"Meet me at the Channel Marina in Richmond at 9:30 a.m." he had said. "We'll embark from there."

To reach the Channel Marina I passed through endlessly sprawling and slummy industrial lands. I was appalled at the waste of land, at the evidence of misuse of land. Here, for sale in the Bay Area, were hundreds of filled acres of bay, which had been in use less than ten years ago by industry. Now, as hideous as any bombed-out city destroyed by war, they lie idle. Industry doesn't want them anymore.

Within six minutes after we left the Channel Marina, our boat docked on Brooks Island. It was the bright fair land that is the California dream, a paradise as yet unbesmirched. Off to the right Canada geese were rising from a long sandspit. A twinkle of sandpipers flitted along a beach any child would love. Shorebirds were calling from the pickleweed marsh of a tide flat. We walked along the shore toward Brooks Island's hill and soon came upon an Indian mound. In the layers of this kitchen-midden, archeologists were painstakingly tracing out the pre-existing culture. For 4000 years human beings had lived on Brooks Island, thriving on the cockles, mussels, oysters, on game, fish and vegetation, without damage to the land. Now, a hundred and thirty years after the heavy hand of "the Gringo" had touched down, one could look in any direction and just beyond the surrounding water there was ugliness and devastation.

It was only the week before that I had seen a new factory set down into the precious vineyard land of Sonoma county. Despite its handsome landscaping, that factory has a doomsday feel to me. It heralds the death of the sweet land surrounding it. Factories and their acres of parking lots have long since consumed the prune and almond orchards of Santa Clara county. Now they are stalking Sonoma county in a ridiculous chase after the worker. The worker of course, has moved to what he thought was country in the first place, trying to escape in his automobile the factory-slums of the city. This is what suburban tracts are all about. Escape from industrial and commercial ugliness. Until there is nowhere left to escape to, for the high tension electrical wires of industry have even intruded into our parks and preserves.

What is it that has made us at once so greedy and so wasteful of land? Only our ignorance.

What makes us exploit nature so selfishly? Only our inability to perceive the consequences.

How can we treat this lush land that is California so dismally, so dangerously? Our selfish profit-motive, to use a more digestible euphemism than the ugly old Anglo-Saxon word, greed. Make no mistake. The great industrialists are already threatening us in the pocketbook. We can clean up the environment, they say, but it will cost you, the consumer.

As I stood on the Brooks Island shore, I suddenly realized that here, emerging, is a new pornography. Something is being hidden under the table. As the Victorian Age made sex obscene, so the Automotive Age, our own culture, is pretending that if we do not look at man's depredations, they don't exist. I blushed for shame for my arrogant race. No Mongolian horde ever wreaked such permanent damage on the land and sky as we. No plague of locusts ever lay waste such acreage irreparably as one could see all about.

A man in a car, insulated from reality, is too busy avoiding instant danger on the freeway, to have time for safe reflection. It takes reflection to understand the displacement of man's responsibility to the environment and what it really means. He isn't about to develop an ecological appreciation (especially when lumbermen leave a 300-foot cosmetic roadside border of trees to hide the slash and erosion) much less an ecological conscience, until he shucks his two-ton, four-wheeled insulation. It is only when a man gets out on foot to walk in intimacy with the land that the ancient tribal memories return. How long since most motorists have smelled a fresh sea breeze clean upon their faces, or sensed the instant pungency of a bay tree in the sun?

With these thoughts heavy upon me, I took a step up the hill. The climb to the top of Brooks Island, like any climb, was harder walking than the beach. But as I climbed, quail ran. A pheasant flew heavily, flashing in the sunlight. The scent of chamomile came up from the grass. A garter snake wriggled off the path. A lark called.

Soon I felt refreshed, invigorated, for walking is a healer too. Like sleep, it mends us up, repairs our minds, renews our strength. By the time I got in the boat to return, my mind was full of resolve, keen to take up the good fight again.

As we chugged back into the shore wasteland, I was reminded of Marston Bates who said "In defying nature, in destroying nature, in building an arrogantly selfish, man-centered artificial world, I do not see how man can gain peace, or freedom, or joy."

Like Dr. Bates "I have faith in man's future, faith in the possibilities latent in the human experiment: but it is faith in man as a part of nature, working with the forces that govern the forests and the seas; faith in man sharing life, not destroying it."

Mine is a faith in man removed from his production-line conquerer's chariot. The man who understands we have only this one world to live in is man standing on the land in his own skin. On his own two feet. Sensing, smelling, seeing, feeling, tasting, touching. It is natural man. The walker.

Margot Patterson Doss
May 7, 1970

Contents

North Bay

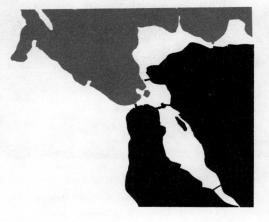

1

Hospital Cove on Angel Island was once the Ellis Island of the West. Now boats lie at anchor, picnickers lounge on the lawns and civilization is a time-lag away.

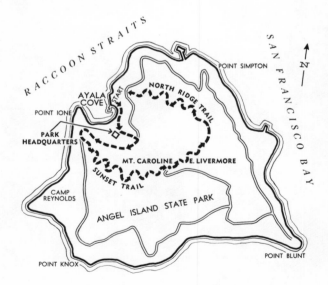

To the Top of Angel Island

■ The boss trail of Angel Island State Park is a climb called Sunset Trail to the peak of Mount Caroline E. Livermore, at 781 feet the summit of the island and blessed with a unique 360-degree view. It is a place of unspoiled beauty, redolent of the long history of the bay, ghostly in the fog and full of new perspective in the sunlight.

For those who are sound of wind and limb, the climb can be a nearby one-day escape from city pressures back into a more pleasant yesterday when people were fewer, motorcars were a rarity and space and the time to enjoy it were every man's prerogative.

To make this walk, get out your hiking boots, for the terrain underfoot on Angel Island is similar to the slopes of Mount Tamalpais. Pack a picnic lunch in your pocket or knapsack and head for the Tiburon or San Francisco ferry docks. Bring a sweater, but skip the swim trunks, for the boats which anchor in Ayala Cove have polluted the graceful curving beach.

Better take along this book, too. Those handy descriptive leaflets once issued all comers as they plunked down their 25-cent admission fee are often in short supply in state parks.

As your ferry puts into Ayala Cove, let your imagination take you back in time to 1775 when Don Juan Manuel de Ayala anchored the Spanish ship *San Carlos* here. From this haven, he spent 40 days exploring and charting the bay. The name he bestowed on the island was the Spanish version of what it is to this day, Isla de los Angeles. Of the names Ayala gave local landmarks only Angel and Alcatraz survive.

Two tule canoes full of Indians came across Raccoon Strait to visit Ayala on August 23, and were entertained aboard his ship.

Once ashore, notice the white building facing the beach beyond the broad lawn. Now park headquarters, this was formerly the U.S. Quarantine Station, which gave the name of Hospital Cove to the area when this was the Ellis Island of the West. Walk toward it (you will pass the elephant train station en route), then take the trail behind the building that goes uphill northeasterly between two wells and a picnic area.

At the highpoint of the road, a larger road crosses it like a T. Check the new trail signs here for distances, then bear right, or southwesterly toward Camp Reynolds. The Sunset Trail takes off on the uphill side of the road above Point Ione, the southern arm of Ayala Cove.

As you swing back and forth on the many switchbacks of Sunset Trail, watch for deer, which have been observed swimming across Raccoon Strait. Caroline E. Livermore, the noted Marin county conservationist for whom this peak, once called Mount Ida, was renamed, would have been gratified to know that 83 species of birds have been spotted here. Wildflowers were seeded in 1920 by the California Spring Blossom and Wildflower Society at the urging of botanist Alice Eastwood, but many of the unusual plants on the island, including the casuarina trees, were introduced by gardeners when Old Fort McDowell and the three other Army garrisons were occupied.

In its time Angel Island has been a prison, an immigration station, a fortified harbor defense and an overseas military staging area. It is possible that it could again become active, as an anti-missile missile base.

From the peak, look toward San Francisco to locate Point Blunt, the U.S. Coast Guard Station located on that portion of the island which is located in San Francisco County. This was the site in 1858 of a duel between Senator William I.

Ferguson, who died of his wounds, and Commissioner George Penn Johnson, author of the anti-dueling law. They fought over the issue of slavery.

When you have surveyed the 640 acres, or one square mile, of this hospitable island park, rest, bask in the sunshine, or picnic before looping back via the North Ridge Trail from the summit for a new set of views of Marin County on the way down.

Ferry Schedule

From Fisherman's Wharf: The Harbor Tours Ferry sails for Angel Island hourly on weekends and holidays between 10 a.m. and 3:45 p.m. through Labor Day. Later in the fall, trips are fewer. Phone 362-5414 to make reservations for large groups, or for weekday schedules.

From Tiburon: Harbor Tours Ferry from 9:30 a.m. through 4:30 p.m.

The McDonough shuttle ferry goes on request from 9 a.m. to 7 p.m. Phone 435-1094 for schedules or reservations. Either Tiburon ferry will schedule an interim trip on two hour's notice or for five or more passengers.

2

Bonita Light is approached via a tunnel and wooden suspension bridge. Visits must be prearranged with the Coast Guard.

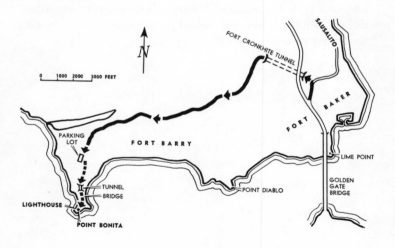

Guardian of the Gate

- Bonita Light!

The name alone is enough to send thrills of high adventure down the spine of anyone who has walked out to it on "a windy day with the white clouds flying, and the flung spray, and the blown spume, and the sea-gulls crying."

For Bonita Light, romantic, snug sentimental sentinel at the Golden Gate's dangerous northeast gatepost, is not only beyond compare for the splendor of its distant vistas and the savagery of abrupt headlands meeting the relentless sea, it is also unique for its foot-trail approach.

The time to make this walk is on one of those blue and gold days on which the light reveals roads etched like scars on the voluptuous bare headlands. To visit it, call public information of the Coast Guard 556-0669, and set up a date for your group.

Like Marin County itself, the best way to get there is through a tunnel and a suspension bridge.

Take the Sausalito turnoff north of Vista Point, then swing off at the sign indicating Forts Barry and Cronkhite. In a trice you will be waiting for the slow signal that admits one-way traffic through the half-mile-long Fort Cronkhite tunnel under Highway 101. Soon it will be a main road to the Golden Gate Headlands State Park. Look uphill to see the larger Waldo tunnels plunge into the ridge.

Once through the Fort Cronkhite tunnel you are immediately in wild wonderful rangeland, which may disappear eventually in the proposed Marincello project.

Drive left, or west. The road leads through a valley along

a stream-bank thick with willows, past military housing and a rifle range. The road forks at Rodeo Lagoon (part of whose shoreline Marincello has already planned as a corporation yard, to the dismay of park planners). Take the uphill road south past the church and watch for a sign indicating the U.S. Coast Guard Station at Point Bonita.

Then drive past missile sites and other Fort Barry installations ever more southerly until a stunning panorama unfolds with the Golden Gate Bridge in the middle distance, San Francisco behind it, and in the northerly foreground, the charming white buildings of the light station.

You have arrived on Point Bonita, a thin gnarled finger of sea-worn rock that is the southernmost point of land in Marin County. If the going has seemed perilous thus far, hold on to your hat.

Park and go down a flight of steps to the three-foot-wide paved trail. Before you reach the lighthouse, a crooked half-mile away, there are eroded cliffs, sheer overhangs, the low tunnel hewn long ago by Chinese coolies working with picks and crude black powder, and two bridges, one the 165-foot suspension bridge that is reputed to be a wooden counterpart of the Golden Gate Bridge.

As you walk downhill, the boat landings below reveal a former lifeboat station, scene of more than one heroic episode. None was more exciting than the time in January 1915 when the steamer *Eureka*, 315 tons, fouled her propeller with a rope out in the four fathom bank of Potato Patch shoals and drifted helplessly onto the rocks.

A surfman, Al Fisher, patrolling the frightening cliffs above Bonita Light, saw her crash and alerted the lighthouse where assistant keeper Alex Martin let himself down in the dark to the ship on 100 feet of rope, only to find he was dangling 50 feet too high. He went back up the rope for more help and returned to save all aboard but one man who went back to the ship for something he'd forgotten.

A cannon, now on display at the Coast Guard base in

Alameda, was the first fog signal here. Manned by a Sergeant Maloney, who found it rough going, the cannon was fired every half hour during fog, until the first light replaced it in 1855. It stood higher than the present light at an elevation of 324 feet.

Since 1877 the light has been 124 feet above water so the beam can be glimpsed under the high-riding fogs. The present light produces 40,000 candlepower and is visible 17 miles at sea. As many a homebound mariner can tell you, it flashes one second, eclipses two, flashes two and eclipses 15. The horn, a super tyfon, which has been compared to a sea-gull's shriek, has a two-second blast, two-second silence, two-second blast, then 24 seconds of silence.

This is a very precarious walk, but one that is rewarding for the walker willing to make the effort.

Seastacks along the coast from the Point Bonita overlook seem as rugged, wild and remote as the Oregon Coast.

3

This overlook by the Sausalito Firehouse makes a great place for spotting the herring run in Richardson Bay. Look for a riot of gulls.

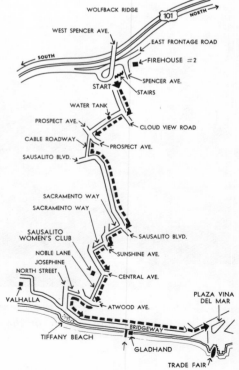

Sausalito Is for Walkers

■ "Browning can have England," the little man in salt-bleached denims in the No Name Bar said. "For me, it's Oh to be in Sausalito when the herring run."

"Tourists are bad enough," replied his companion with no little disgust. "But herring! The stink, man! Who can stand it?"

The happy citizens of Sausalito can stand it and most of them love the annual day or two of excitement that is generated when the Pacific herring come in to Richardson Bay to spawn.

Sausalito is a walker's town (as well as being a sailor's town, a painter's town, a poet's town, a shopper's town, a potter's town, a browser's town and a good place to spend a weekend). It offers interesting walking at any time, but when the herring run . . . .

Ah, when the herring run, the sky is alive with wheeling, screaming sea birds, and the shore with barefoot kids. The water churns with fish and spermy strings of eggs, and harbor seals gorge themselves like Hogarthian peasants at a county fair.

Happy pelicans prove their bellies can hold what their beaks can, and sometimes flop in the water from too much ballast. The blustery air is keen, even heady with what Herb Beckman of The Tides bookstore described as "an unmistakably Dionysian and nostril-dilating odor." The tempo of the town, otherwise a little sleepy, suddenly becomes *Rites of Spring, con brio.*

The time of year to take this walk is along about mid-

January. If you have a friend in Sausalito, ask him to send up a smoke signal. On the great day, park your car alongside the attractive brown-shingled Sausalito Firehouse Number 2, easily accessible from Highway 101 via the Spencer-Monte Mar turnoff. Northbound Greyhound locals let passengers off here on request.

Make a herring reconnaissance of Richardson Bay looking north from the phone booth. A cloud of gulls is the giveaway. If you see them, follow Spencer downhill in that direction. If not, climb the stairs across the street from the firehouse and skirt the approach to Wolfback overpass until you are parallel with the dead-end bollards of Cloud View Road.

On Cloud View walk downhill about a block, past a pleasing variety of hill-top homes. At the stone wall, go south for a few yards. Suddenly it is a country road near a water tank. Climb up the berm by the tank for a breathtaking view of Wolfback Ridge above. To the southeast is the City, the Bay Bridge, the East Bay, and in the middle water, Alcatraz, looking like a fat ship. From this vantage, gulls in the bay may show progress of a school of herring, too.

The downhill route is well outlined on the hillside for a few hundred yards, ending near a sign saying, "Channing Way." Turn away downhill instead and look for the sign across the road which says "Cable Roadway." This is one of Sausalito's charming pedestrian lanes, built by the Sausalito Land and Ferry Company in the days when developers understood their civic duties. Next to the brown-shingled house that says "Treacy 39," the lane becomes a staircase with iron handrails. Go down through the trees and ivy, watching for tantalizing glimpses of the water below. This is old Sausalito at her informal fishing-village best.

When a road intervenes, bear left to the junction of Crescent and Sausalito Boulevards. Take Sausalito, and stay on it beyond Sunshine, until you pass number 652, a white house with large terra cotta pineapples on the overdoor. The steps of Sacramento Way, another pleasant lane, go down just beyond the hedge. At Sunshine revisited, bear left downhill for about 75 feet to a sign indicating the continuance of Sacramento Way. It goes down by a house whose sign warns "Beware of the Cat."

At Central, bear left again, past wonderful old houses until you reach the Sausalito Women's Club, designed by architect Julia Morgan, who also built Hearst's Castle in San Simeon. There is a pleasant bench on which to rest here, near a plaque dedicated to Grace McGregor Robbins.

Pick up Noble Lane, just downhill alongside the fence saying "37." From this gentle ramp, there is an intimate view of Raccoon Strait outlined by Angel Island and Belvedere. Children hug the pine tree in the middle of the steps as they pass. At Atwood, bear right to Josephine, to the concrete pillars indicating North Street. This too is a lane. Two-thirds of the way down is another welcome bench that looks on sandy Tiffany Beach below, with Al Cebrian's sleek seal offshore. A few more steps and there you are on Bridgeway in the Sausalito of Sally Stanford's Valhalla restaurant.

First-time visitors might feel impelled to walk toward the Valhalla to find the town. They would have been right in 1849 when whalers put into Shelter Cove for water and beef here at the base of Hurricane Gulch. Today the center of commerce is farther north along the waterfront. Walk north toward the restaurants jutting into the water.

To board the bus back to the City, or to find a taxi which will take you up to the firehouse for your car, follow the shoreline to Plaza Vina del Mar, once El Portal Park, and now renamed for Sausalito's Chilean sister village. Here the obvious pleasures of Sausalito are on every hand for the visitor to discover for himself.

If you missed the herring run, try again next year. You'll have seen the real Sausalito, and have had a pleasant walk, with or without herring.

4
___

*Fort Cronkhite will one day be part of the Golden Gate
Headlands State Park. William Antonio Richardson, San
Francisco's first settler, once rounded up cattle here.*

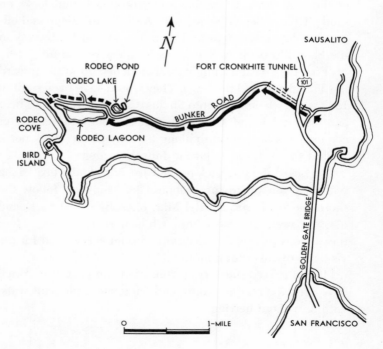

Quiet Lagoons in Marin

■ Rodeo Lagoon is not one, but three, secret silver-blue lakes, whose beauty like that of the human face, changes from moment to moment. They lie in a hollow of land where the southern-most mountains of Marin go down to the sea. In time, it is their happy destiny to become the important central part of the Golden Gate Headlands State Park.

The walking around them is interesting indeed, for few places so near the City have been, until now, so relatively undisturbed.

To make this walk, take the Sausalito turnoff north of Vista Point and quickly turn left at the Bunker Road entrance to Forts Barry and Cronkhite. In a moment you will reach a tunnel one-half mile long under Highway 101. The entrance is controlled by automatic lights that admit cars in one-way caravans.

This will one day be the main entrance to the headlands park. Once through the tunnel, follow Bunker Road west as it borders the willows that hide Rodeo Creek until you are in sight of a little red-roofed chapel. Pull off across the road that goes between two of the lakes, park, and follow the red-rock path bordering the road.

Within 100 yards, the walker will find himself abreast of a break in the willows that leads to a tongue of land with a raft and fishing pier abutting it. Walk out on it and you are between the two uppermost lakes.

The Army, on whose land 94% of the lagoons are situated, distinguishes the middle-sized one by calling it Rodeo Lake. Rodeo Pond is the smallest, Rodeo Lagoon the largest. All three lakes, Rodeo Cove and Rodeo Avenue in Sausalito derive their name from Don William Antonio Richardson's Rancho Sausalito cattle sales, held here after 1835 when he bought the ranch from one of Anza's soldiers, Nicolas Galindo of Durango.

Helen Van Cleave Park, a Mill Valley historian and authority on Richardson, has found a reference in which "Richardson and a party of hunters started up a band of elk, seven bear and three cubs" nearby. The Rodeo Lagoon name was well established by the time Van Dorn published his Marin County rancho map of 1860.

Drop a line in the water of the upper lakes and you may catch a trout. The State Department of Fish and Game has been stocking the freshwater lakes since 1957. Fish in Rodeo Lagoon, across the road, and you may catch a bass instead. Bass fingerlings were stocked here for the first time in the fall of '65.

As stream-fed seaside lakes often are, these waters seem fickle. Willis Evans, who made the original fish and game survey of the lagoons in 1953, says this is not as mysterious as it seems. Close to the source, Rodeo Creek, the water is sweet and has been used as an auxiliary reservoir by the military (non-drinking purposes only). Close to the sea, the water is salty.

Look north to see a carpet of wildflowers on the beautiful bare hillside on the opposite shore. This is the old Silva ranch now proposed for the controversial Marincello development. Park planners are dismayed to learn bulldozers have already changed the upstream ecology by removing streamside willows and brush needed to sustain fish life.

When you have searched for nesting marshbirds and raccoon pawprints, follow the road across the dam to see screens that protect trout from wandering into the wrong body of water. Long ago steelhead came up Rodeo Creek to spawn.

Then continue around the border of the larger lagoon

toward the Pacific Ocean, passing the Fort Cronkhite military housing, to reach the gravelly beach between Bird Island Point and Tennessee Point that defines Rodeo Cove. Anglers treasure it for surf-fishing, rock-fishing and mussels. Bird watchers like it for the variety of shore and waterfowl. But to the rockhound, Cronkhite Beach is Mecca, for it is here that he can find gem quality carnelians, jade, chalcedony and jasper pebbles washed smooth by the sea.

Children are sheltered from the surf by a long sand box closing the lagoon mouth. Rockhounds hunt the beach pebbles for jasper, jade and carnelians.

*From the southern tip of Belvedere, the Golden Gate Bridge
seems isolated and final. Deep watermen once brought cod
fish through the gate for processing at Belvedere's only industry, a codfishery.*

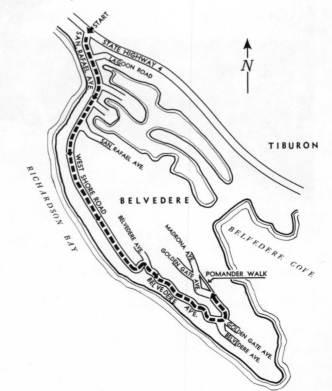

A Lane in Belvedere

■ Pomander Walk is a country lane that rides the crest of beautiful Belvedere. Tall hedgerows define it. Blooming vines entwine it. The linnets twitter as they flit along it.

At any moment Greer Garson, in the role of Mrs. Miniver, might come hurrying out of the swinging gate at Number 2 Pomander, bound perhaps to a fund-raiser for a worthy cause.

If you have never walked around Belvedere, you've missed one of the Bay Area's most exotic experiences. This is the densely-packed, Riviera-like community that launched lagoon-living, suburbia's best antidote to the unimaginative tract.

Begin this excursion at the juncture of Highway 4 and San Rafael Avenue. (This is also a bus stop.) Walk southwest across the Northwestern Pacific tracks. In 1882, these were built by the San Francisco and North Pacific Railroad, popularly known as the "Donahue Line" and as "The Irishman's Railroad," for owner James M. Donahue whose ferries to San Francisco raced a rival line out of Sausalito.

Follow San Rafael Avenue and in a trice the street is out of the trees and bordering the shoreline of Richardson Bay, where a narrow, park-like promenade is now emerging, complete with six benches placed at intervals for bird or moon-watching.

Bear consistently right, or west, pausing at the floodgate for a look at the Belvedere lagoon, the only viewpoint accessible to the public from this northern spit. In the 1880s houseboat dwellers, who called themselves "the Venetians of the

West," and "Descendants of Noah" brought arks to winter in this sheltered cove, making a procession through a comparable floodgate in the southern spit, now Beach Road.

It was then called Hilarita's Spit, for Hilarita Sanchez, whose name saint is commemorated in St. Hilary's church, the charming landmark uphill on the eastern ridge.

San Rafael Avenue soon turns, following the lagoon to the yacht club, Belvedere Land Company, and municipal offices and passing, en route, the award-winning Christian Science church designed by Warren Callister.

For this walk, however, to see how Belvedere is evolving, continue along the water's edge, bearing right on West Shore Road. The cliff above is known as Britton Ridge.

As you pass 8-10 West Shore Road, once a Pacific Heights mansion which was floated over from San Francisco on two barges, notice the gray and white layers in the cliff behind. This was one of the many Marin Indian shell mounds. Viewpoints, open to the water, have been left for the delight of walkers.

If you can take your eyes away from the splendor of Sausalito, its hills and the Golden Gate Bridge, look landward across from 83, to see steps in the cliff. From here to the end of the road was once the site of Belvedere's lone industry, the codfishery of T. W. McCollam. Around 1875, great four-masted sailing ships brought their cargo here to the Union Fish Company's long wharf and curing sheds.

Zig-zag uphill to Belvedere Avenue, then bear south to Pine, swinging back to Golden Gate to find Pomander Walk. It is hard today to envision the burly codfishermen climbing up and over this spine of land to spend their money in the raucous bars of Sharktown, as Tiburon was then known.

It's equally difficult to believe a man named Israel Kashaw once tried to prove this was an island, but there's still a pear tree from his orchard near the corner of Laurel and San Rafael Avenues, if you care to hunt it out.

28

Looking toward Corinthian Island from one of the many pedestrian lanes in Belvedere. Town planners provided lanes for easy ferry boat access to residents who commuted in comfort.

Tiburon is a yachting town and a great place to visit by ferry boat today.

Tiburon—Sharktown at Line's End

■ The non-town of Tiburon, whose melodic name is Spanish for "shark," is a community at the southern tip of the Marin County peninsula of the same name, largely populated by people who would rather look at San Francisco than live in it. Traditionally, it has been a resort for seafarers and bayfarers.

Wayfarers will also find the exploring in Tiburon exceptional for two reasons: Old St. Hilary's garden of wildflowers which boasts the black jewel flower and the Tiburon paintbrush, not known to exist anywhere else in the world. There are also freight yards of what was once the southern terminus of the San Francisco and North Pacific Railroad.

Begin this walk at the Tiburon Greyhound bus stop, an undistinguished little shanty on Tiburon Boulevard with its back to the railroad tracks. Save the commercial attractions of Main Street, a showcase for paint czar Fred Zelinsky, until the end of this excursion. Walk for the nonce toward the ferry slip built originally in 1884 by Peter Donahue, the pioneer blacksmith who also built San Francisco's first foundry, the Union Iron Works, and gave the City its first gas lights.

Before you reach the slip, if you can tear your eyes away from the unbelievable panorama of San Francisco Bay from this point, notice on your left the row houses beyond the valley, once a railroad owned "company town." Until the railroad came, this peninsula was a hilly pastureland, part of Rancho Corte Madera del Presidio, whose name merely means "cut wood for the Presidio."

It was granted in 1834 to John Thomas Reed and his wife, Ylaria Sanchez, on the condition that they build a sawmill and supply the San Francisco Presidio with wood. The nearby towns of Mill Valley and Corte Madera, where Reed built his mill and cut the wood, take their names from this grant.

Toward Angel Island, the point of land fenced off for fishing is Elephant Rock, a spot reserved for children. Around the curve from it is an odd little round building called Lyford's Tower. Dr. Benjamin Lyford, who married one of Reed's daughters, Hilarita, aspired to build a health farm here.

Once across the tracks, bear left and parallel the tracks until you reach Reed School. This is the corner of Mar West and Esperanza. Walk uphill on Esperanza, then Alemany, until you see the simple white church that is Old St. Hilary's on its eminence.

This charming old place of worship was built in 1888 by Dr. Lyford and his wife over a spring reputed to have been responsible for at least one miraculous cure. The spring bubbles up from the front staircase to this day, on what was once part of the old Spanish Trail. (Look for the stone wall that circles the church on the north for more of the old trail.)

The water seeping down the stairs makes a marshy strip whose "fingers" nurture some of the exciting botanical rarities for which this little preserve is known. John Thomas Howell, curator-emeritus of botany at the California Academy of Sciences, has listed at least eleven species indigenous to this knoll, and calls it a "floral diadem." The procedure to save it is so simple, he says, it probably won't be followed.

"It must not be disturbed, landscaped, planted, weeded, irrigated or walked on," Howell insists. "What nature has created through a millenium, man might destroy in a day by 'improvements.'"

When you have explored Old St. Hilary's, retrace your steps to the bus stop, or to Main Street. A ferry to Angel Island leaves from the Tiburon Ferry dock. "Folk-art"

establishments abound along Main Street and invite brows-
ing if you have allowed yourself time and are in the mood.

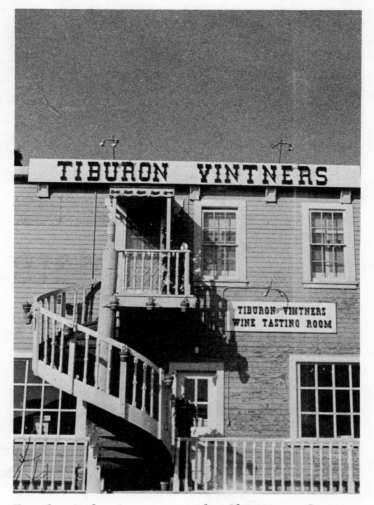

*For thousands of romantics, the Champagne Cruise to
Tiburon aboard a Harbor Tour boat, has an added filip in
the tasting rooms of Tiburon Vintners, housed in this Victorian with a flamboyant staircase.*

7

The Mount Tamalpais and Muir Woods railway trains used to go through a gap in this Mill Valley street.

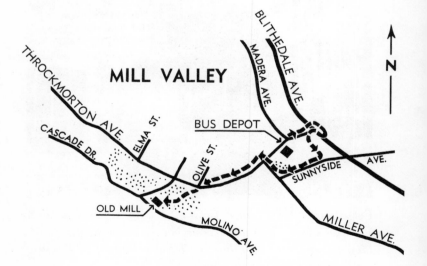

Mill Valley Shows the Way

■ Downtown Mill Valley has more genuine charm per square foot than most other Bay Area towns. A walk around it can be one of the pleasantest experiences this side of 1920.

To make this walk, begin at the Greyhound bus depot, at Miller and Throckmorton Avenues. Originally this subtly painted arched building was a railroad station where commuters boarded the electric trains for the Sausalito ferry and the tourists got on the Mount Tamalpais and Muir Woods Railway for the wonderfully convoluted ride to the peak of Mount Tamalpais. You can still see the electric train rails in what is now the parking lot.

Better still, envision great open tracts of pastureland lying between this redwood valley and Sausalito, where San Franciscans left the ferry to board the big orange electric train and make the steam mountain train connection here. Heartier souls often came as walking clubs to make on foot the trip from the ferry to the top of Tamalpais, for Mill Valley years ago was a summer resort.

The bus depot now houses an excellent bookstore and the most enlightened Chamber of Commerce in the Bay Area. It stands on Lytton Square, named for Lytton Barber, Mill Valley's first World War I casualty.

Look all directions to see how pleasantly the earth colors harmonize, how discreet the signs are.

From the Throckmorton side of the bus depot, bear right and at the junction with Madera Avenue right again, away from the Mill Valley Market. Shortly you will find yourself at El Paseo, an informal grouping of shops designed by Gus

Costigan for Edna Foster. World travelers will be reminded of Spain or Mexico. This is one of several such El Paseos in the Bay Area and it houses two unique places.

One is The Nature Store, devoted to museum-quality ecological specimens, the other Mary Hoskin's El Paseo Restaurant (open 6 to 11, Thursday through Sunday only), where the popovers are so good they have blossomed into a widely marketed gourmet frozen-food item. Continue on to 6 Throckmorton at the corner of East Blithedale Avenue, to see the old brown-shingled Maybeck building which houses the Mill Valley Outdoor Art Club. A memorial garden encloses it.

Across the way is the striking Mount Carmel Roman Catholic Church, built in 1968 and designed by architect Fred P. Houweling. Also worth noting nearby are Pumas Books, an entrancing shop, its neighbor, The Art Store, and the Lady Baltimore Bakery, which sometimes has a sign in the window announcing "apple pan dowdy."

When you have explored these, return to El Paseo, which has a pleasant winding shortcut through to Sunnyside Avenue. Take a right downhill past the brown-shingled building with its round tower and window full of books to reach some redwoods beside a creek. This has been trenched with rocks, which makes it less formidably ugly than the concrete trenches built in Marin County by the Corps of Engineers.

Soon you are at Miller Avenue again. Those two center islands of redwoods may be the smallest park in the world, but park they are, complete with bench.

If this is your first visit to Mill Valley, round out this walk with an inspection of the Old Mill Park, in which part of the mill that gave Mill Valley its name still stands. To reach it, bear right on Miller to Throckmorton, then left on Throckmorton (making your own discoveries of the interesting shops en route) until you reach Old Mill Street.

Walk left, into the great cathedral of trees to find the mill structure, where John Reed began milling lumber in 1834.

Shady ways and vernal charm are Mill Valley's great attraction. When Highway 101 bypassed the Valley it created a quiet oasis where the living is lovely.

8

In Muir Woods the fingerlings still come up into Redwood Creek and Fern Creek. Woodwardia ferns and bracken festoon the rocks and blue forget-me-nots bloom in the springtime under the redwoods.

The Red Trees of Muir Woods

■ The redwoods, tallest conifers in the world, are so elusive
that white men did not see them for more than 200 years
after the discovery of California. The credit for finding them,
according to Norman Taylor in his book *The Ageless Relicts*,
goes jointly to Fray Juan Crespi and Miguel Costanso of the
Portola expedition.

In October of 1769, both described in their journals the
trees they noted on the Pajaro River flowing into Monterey
Bay. "Because none of the expedition recognizes them, they
are named red wood from their color," wrote Crespi, so
linking tree and name on the spot.

"Actually what Crespi saw was a relatively small stand
of this fabulous evergreen," Taylor explains, "which does not
become common until one reaches the San Francisco Bay
area."

The most famous stand remaining in the Bay Area, as
half the world knows, is Muir Woods. It is a rare and awe-
some experience to walk alone among the redwoods. More
than half a million people walk through Muir Woods annually (a number that would astonish both naturalist John
Muir, for whom the grove is named, and Congressman William Kent, who gave the redwood canyon to the people of
the United States).

Ninety per cent of the visitors don't get off the canyon
floor. Most of them make only the short loop of the nature
trail, a walk that can be completed in ten minutes. Some follow the main trail to Bohemian Grove or to Cathedral Grove.
Few indeed are those who experience in silence, away from

the crowds, that unique and perspective-creating moment of comparison between man and tree.

Crowded as Muir Woods is (to the point where rangers regard the visitor as a menace and are apt to dwell on the subject of human erosion), it is still possible to walk quietly and alone among the redwoods. The way to do it is simple. Go on a weekday and get up on the hillsides.

Begin this walk by dressing appropriately for mountain trails, preferably in sturdy walking boots. Tuck an apple or chocolate bar into your pocket and go, secure in the knowledge that Kent meant his gift to be both conserved and enjoyed. During his lifetime, the Mount Tamalpais and Muir Woods Railway, of which he was an officer, ran "self-propelled" gravity cars on a spur track down the side of "Mount Tam" to Muir Woods. Thousands of visitors came coasting down, the ladies squealing on the turns, in open cars now regarded as a railroad oddity.

Botanical oddities are more frequent in Muir Woods today. Among them are albino shoots of redwood trees, and the burnt ghosts, some attached to living trees. As you come through the entrance barricades, pick up a Muir Woods National Monument folder, which contains a map—and an explanation of what a burnt ghost is.

Botanists may also wish to stop at the visitors center to purchase *Flowers and Ferns of Muir Woods* by Gladys Smith, published by the Muir Woods Natural History Association. It also has a map. Follow the main trail along the north side of Redwood Creek. The wire-encaged tree you pass is a dawn redwood. Packrats, rather than deer or people, made the cage necessary.

Before you cross Fern Creek, take a short side trip to the Kent Memorial, a marker that commemorates the conservationist who purchased this land in 1908 to prevent a water company from turning the irreplaceable grove into a reservoir. It was the first of our national monuments.

Return to the main trail until it merges with Bootjack

Trail. Continue on Bootjack to Ben Johnson Trail, which joins Hillside Trail and rambles along the south canyon wall above Redwood Creek. It comes out at the Bohemian Grove, making a pleasant loop. You may be surprised at how lonely this walk can be.

The Redwoods with their cathedral-like quality give man a new perspective.

9

Rocky Point, where the Steep Ravine Trail ends by the Sundown Sea, as Indians called the Pacific Ocean, overlooked a natural hot spring until earthquake action closed it. Hikers, but not automobiles, can go down on the marine meadow and beach below.

MT. TAMALPAIS STATE PARK

RIDGECREST BLVD.

BOOTJACK CAMP

PANORAMIC HIGHWAY

BOLINAS RIDGE HIGHWAY

N

SOUTHSIDE ROAD

PAN TOLL CAMP
RANGER STATION

DAVIS TRAIL

MATT

STEEP RAVINE TRAIL

STINSON BEACH

STINSON BEACH HIGHWAY

DIPSEA TRAIL

WEBB CREEK

PACIFIC OCEAN

Remote and Mysterious Steep Ravine

■ Steep Ravine, an almost unbelievable wilderness canyon carved through several geologic ages by a sea-eager rivulet called Webb Creek, lies, as commuters tell time, thirty minutes from San Francisco, on the western face of Mount Tamalpais. Through it runs a hiker's mountain trail with a mysterious built-in magic of its own, a lesson to teach the perceptive, and for those walkers who like it, symbolism.

The trip through Steep Ravine begins on Matt Davis Trail in Bootjack Camp of Mount Tamalpais State Park. Look for the marker at the lower end of the parking lot across the road from the Pan Toll Ranger Station. If you're going to hike it alone, the ranger will appreciate it if you let him know, just before you start.

As mountaineers judge trails, this is an easy one, a lady's walk, but there are places where it is wet, slick and treacherous. There are also two ladders to scramble. The temptation is to say that Steep Ravine is for the young, sound and vigorous. Nevertheless, it was a trio of remarkable grandmothers—Mrs. Harry B. Allen, Mrs. Edward Bosqui and Mrs. Morley Thompson Whitehouse—who led me for the first time down this other-worldly mountain path.

They were dressed for the occasion and had worn waterproof "birdshooter" boots with a slight heel that proved better on the trail than my own low sneakers. Just before we began, Mrs. Allen distributed walking sticks, one of which was a Malacca "lawyer" used in the country of its origin for "beating the truth" out of debtors. On this trip a stout stick is no affectation.

A bare trickle of water dripped down near the trail's beginning as we started, and burbled its way between the great redwood and fir trees that grow in this narrow ravine. It was dark, coming in out of the blue and gold sunshine, with dapples of sunlight filtering lacily through high branches. Soon another stream joined and broadened the creek making a duet of waters whose music swelled in the silence like a living presence.

The mysterious magic of Steep Ravine is its silence, and its illusion of remoteness. Panoramic Highway also runs through it. Cars may pass but the hiker neither sees nor hears them. From the cars, the motorists, too, are unaware of the hikers. This is also its lesson: That the motor road need not be a destroyer of beauty.

The trail winds around rocks and over fallen trees and, in one place, under a great felled log. Like Muir Woods National Monument just south of Steep Ravine's upper half, this is pristine forest. Great trees such as these once covered all the slopes along Highway 1 throughout the Bolinas-Tomales area. The natural wildflowers of the "juicy" woods give way to hillside. Just beyond the footbridge, baby blue-eyes grow.

Marin conservationists have recently added the last lap of the trail to public park use. Cross Dipsea Trail and follow the creek down toward the sea. It emerges in a seaside meadow at Highway 1, above Rocky Point. Bear north fifty feet or so and cross the road, as Webb Creek does. The gate is locked to auto traffic, except by permission of the Stinson Beach ranger, but walkers may go through.

It is here at Rocky Point that Winifred Allen has found the symbolism she enjoys, where Webb Creek leaps jubilantly to the sea after an adventurous course. "My family has promised to set off a roaring explosion of fireworks here for me, instead of giving me a somber and funereal sendoff when I finally reach the sea," Mrs. Allen says. "It is the most beautiful jumping off place I know."

Webb Creek cascades into Steep Ravine, a canyon that plunges from the shoulders on Mount Tamalpais to the Pacific Ocean below.

10   *On weekdays, hikers can find the silent solitude that is the essence of "the wilderness experience" on many of the Tamalpais trails. State park rules now require dogs to be leashed, so bring a long one.*

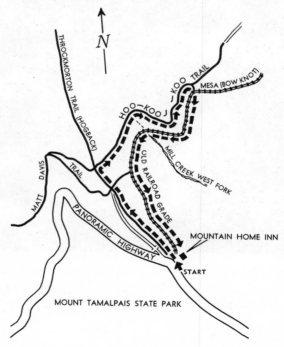

Tamalpais in the Spring

■ It is an old San Francisco tradition "when Spring brings back blue days and fair" to go for a walk on The Mountain.

The Mountain in the San Francisco Bay Area (all claims by the higher Mount Diablo to the contrary notwithstanding) is Mount Tamalpais, elevation 2604 feet, the highest point in Marin County—possibly because its environs are so spectacular.

According to geologist William E. Ver Planck, "Mount Tamalpais, a wall-like ridge that extends northeastward across the southern portion of Marin County, is dissected by steep gorges; and sharp-backed ridges diverge from the summit. The Marin Peninsula is formed by such a ridge that trends southeastward toward the Golden Gate. Within a mile of Lime Point elevations on the ridge crest are nearly 1000 feet."

In other words, "Mount Tam," as it was nicknamed long ago, has its feet in the bay. You are actually walking on Tamalpais at Vista Point and in Sausalito. Tamalpais also has its feet in the Pacific Ocean. A walk on the mountain could begin as easily in Mill Valley or Stinson Beach. For most walkers (as for cyclists, fishermen, picnickers and other outdoorsmen) in all practicality, The Mountain begins at a point where they feel they have left the urban area behind and are in wilder mountainous country.

Mountain Home Inn on the edge of Mount Tamalpais State Park is such a point. Ten trails converge here. For a choice spring walk overlooking the bay, leave your wheels here. Mountain Home Inn is a bus stop and has parking.

Walk uphill on Throckmorton (Hogback) Trail. Go past the fire station and water tank for a steep 500 feet to the second intersection. The first is Matt Davis Trail, also pleasant.

For this walk, however, turn east at the second trail, Hoo-Koo-E-Koo, named for a non-existent Indian tribe invented by Dan Totheroh, in the play which he wrote for the Mountain Theater in 1921. It has often been performed there since and proceeds have been used to maintain the trail.

At this point Hoo-Koo-E-Koo Trail is wide enough for one person only and walkers will want to go single file. It takes off across the shoulders of "Mount Tam" in waist-high chaparral, mostly manzanita and ceanothus and plunges into a silent forest that surrounds the west fork of Mill Creek.

A walker one might often meet along this trial is Edith Thacher Hurd, author of many children's books, among them *The Day the Sun Danced*. Her husband, Clement Hurd, illustrator of this and others, including the only children's book ever written by Gertrude Stein, has his artist's studio a mile or so away and sometimes works outdoors on The Mountain.

Naturalists can look for two pack rat nests on the trailside, before you reach Mill Creek, which Clement Hurd describes as one of the "intimate creeks" of the mountainside. "Stay well back from the edge of rocky outcroppings," Edith Hurd advises. "One time I took my son and a friend for a walk and was showing them how the rock can break away. 'If you go too close, the rock may split and tumble you downhill,' I said, and the rock split and tumbled me as the words came out of my mouth, dumping me 10 to 15 feet down the slope," she recalls.

Hoo-Koo-E-Koo Trail cuts downhill east of Mesa, in the area known to railroad buffs as the Double Bow Knot, where the Mount Tamalpais and Muir Woods Railway curved around to earn its title, "The Crookedest Railroad in the World." Bear right on the railroad grade.

48

Look for the old cement platform at Mesa, where the trains used to stop. Then turn west, to follow the railroad grade back to the Mountain Home Inn. You may be able to pick up old railroad spikes along the way, souvenirs of the trains that puffed to the top of The Mountain and to Muir Woods until 1930.

As you walk through lovely trees and typical indigenous shrubs, watch for stunning glimpses of San Francisco and the bay in the distance.

This land is now part of the 4796-acre addition to Mount Tamalpais State Park, which will have 238 camp units, 160 picnic units and 31 miles of walking trails.

Pioneer Juan Reed, who built the mill that gave Mill Valley its name, rafted redwood logs to San Francisco down this long estuary of Miller Creek, then through the Bay. The "Crookedest Railroad in the World" also wound down this slope of Mount Tamalpais.

11

This is the view from Tamalpais. It is worth the hike up the old railroad grade to see Mill Valley, the Bay and San Francisco beyond.

The View from Tamalpais

■ For my money, the Twenty-Minute Scenic Trail around the peak of Mount Tamalpais is the most exhilarating walk in the Bay Area. It may well rank with the more beautiful walks of the world.

Good anytime, it is best of all in the fall when ruffled clouds make bunchy lace below it. From the trail one can survey in quick succession all 360 degrees of the compass, yet it is a relatively level walk most anyone can enjoy.

Begin this walk in the free public parking lot on Tamalpais' East Peak. (If you are dependent on public transportation, get off the Bolinas-bound Greyhound bus at Mountain Home Inn and take the steep Throckmorton [Hogback] Trail to the same point. Wear boots.) At the outset, notice the picnic tables in the oaks and pines just north of the parking area. This grove was just below the terminal siding for the Mount Tamalpais and Muir Woods Railway, and winter rains occasionally wash out artifacts of the railroad.

Walk east, toward the still-evident foundations of the old Tamalpais Tavern. Near the new adobe-style restrooms is a sign indicating the Twenty-Minute Trail goes north. Take it. Within a few steps Lake Lagunitas and the larger Bon Tempe Lake are visible. Meadow Golf Club, velvety green, lies beyond to remind the walker that grass, as John Ingalls describes it, is "the forgiveness of nature—her constant benediction."

If you can take your eyes from the splendor of the hilly terrain below, at the first view stop notice the plaque which says "Back to The Mountain in the fullness of life," and gives the dates of George Grant and his Grace Adelaide, who came instead in the emptiness of death. As you walk, star thorn, manzanita, oak and madrone border the trail, framing tantalizing glimpses of San Rafael, the Sir Francis Drake highway and the bay. The next curve reveals Corte Madera Slough, Point San Quentin, the Richmond-San Rafael Bridge and the fields of oil tanks in Richmond.

The East Peak fire trail and the Indian fire trail which peel off below are part of a fire-protection pattern created in 1913 by F. E. Olmsted, of the famous park-planning family.

The face of Mount Tamalpais has been blackened by fire many times. Gardner Lookout, the little tower at its apex, named for Edwin B. Gardner, long Chief Warden of the Tamalpais Fire District, is manned by fire wardens from May 15 each year until the rain gauge registers three inches.

North Knee is the easily accessible viewpoint a few hundred feet down Blithedale Ridge on the Indian fire trail. The latter is a misleading name since Indians shunned the peak as a place of strong magic until a white man challenged them.

According to H. P. Munro-Fraser, the pioneer Jacob Primer Leese first scaled the mountain. Leese found his Indian assistants frightened because "the top of the mountain was inhabited by evil spirits and no one could go up there and come back alive." Leese climbed the mountain and made a cross of branches that could be seen below to disprove it. Not to be outdone, Chief Marin, considered by his men to be the bravest man in the world, then made the climb, and hung his red shirt on the cross. His friends decided he had been "robbed of his uniform by the Devil himself" until he returned.

When the hot summer wind known locally as the "Devil's Breath" roars off the peak, it is easy to see why a primitive people would fear it. To this day Indian shamans perform special rituals with a crystal on the mountaintop every 12 years; they consider Tamalpais one of the three enchanted peaks in California.

Look for hazelnuts near the Devil's Slide, which begins in the forefront of the vast panorama of the east bay. Tamalpa Trail is the next to join the Twenty-Minute Trail. Thereafter the trail footing becomes wooden—old railroad ties set into the cliff. Duck under the big rock outcropping and you're on a little bridge overlooking Tiburon and San Francisco.

A moment or two more and you have arrived at Sunrise Point, with a bench conveniently placed for viewing and steel cables protecting an even more daring overlook. After a soul-filling gaze, end this walk where you began it, having looped the mountain at an elevation of 2400 feet above sea level.

The supreme view from Tamalpais is from Gardener Lookout, a fire watching platform near the top of Mt. Tam.

53

12 *From the south shore of Bon Tempe Lake a hiker can pretend to be in England's Lake Country.*

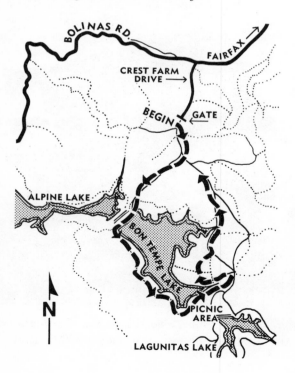

A Walk Around a Marin Lake

■ If you have been citybound too long, try a walk around
Bon Tempe Lake. A four-mile trail, easy enough for octoge-
narians, around Bon Tempe, the middle in a stair-step chain
of Marin Municipal Water District reservoirs, gives the
walker glimpses of its two neighboring lakes, Alpine and
Lagunitas.

To go through the wild country surrounding them is to go
home again to the good sweet earth as it used to be.

Transport yourself to Fairfax via Sir Francis Drake Boulevard to make this walk. Then take Bolinas Road away from
town until you reach a left turn road called Crest Farm Drive.
(If you reach Camp Lilienthal, go back, you have overshot
it.) Follow Crest Farm Drive left as far as you can and park
at the area surrounding the first automotive barrier you
reach. Frequently there are horsetrailers here, for it is a
favorite access point for horsemen.

Walk past the barrier, following the asphalt road (closed
to cars at some seasons) until you reach a signpost which indicates that Bon Tempe and Alpine Lakes are to the right,
Lagunitas to the left. Follow the dirt road to the right and
walk with the music of water, laughing at this season, all the
way to the lake.

Like Disney's "Fantasia," the springtime drip, drip, drip
soon accelerates from trickle to gurgle to rush. It reaches a
crescendo within a quarter of a mile when you reach the
spillway from Bon Tempe into the lower Alpine Lake.

Bear left here, ignoring signs which do not discriminate
between the lake and the trail name, and climb the embank-

ment. Then walk across it. The nets offshore are to protect fish and swimming birds from being swept into the spill. "Don't pull the plug," my son Sandy advised two ducks swimming near the lip, "or you'll drain the lake."

At the end of the levee, bear left into the woods, leaving the road for a footpath through trees, blanketed under moss like children bundled against a storm. The path skirts the water's edge, crossing little feeder creeks and streams on stepping stones and logs. If the sun has been out at all, the ground is rich with tasty mushrooms and other fungi. Watch especially for clavaria, the tasty coral mushroom, for day stars and great shelf mushrooms.

About half way round the lake, just about the time you want to rest and get a drink of water, you'll reach the Lake Lagunitas picnic area, just beyond a water district shed and nursery. Tables and privies and a mapboard make this a logical place to lunch. Lagunitas spillway announces itself by sound.

Then follow the road back around a long finger of the nearby Bon Tempe Lake, taking a hard right, followed by a hard left onto asphalt Lagunitas Road. If instead you would rather continue skirting the lake, follow it along the abandoned road to the water, then go uphill, overland, where many a walker has blazed the cross country route before you. In either case, you'll take the hard road for a quarter of a mile or so along the east side of the lake.

Look for the path again to return to the dam spillway by bearing ever left if you wish to make a continual waterside circuit. Or cut along the asphalt road all the way back to your starting point if you prefer.

En route, you may meet dog walkers exercising their golden retrievers, as we did, or find water district manager Stan Cemiccia happening by at just the right moment to give trail advice. Once you've discovered this enchanting lake country, other parks will seem tame by comparison.

Horsemen enjoy the trail around Bon Tempe Lake. So do walkers, deer and raccoons. Go in the early morning or at dusk to see wild fowl and native fauna by this waterhole.

13

Bolinas Lagoon is bordered on the north by an unpretentious summer colony where the living is natural and 50 years behind the times.

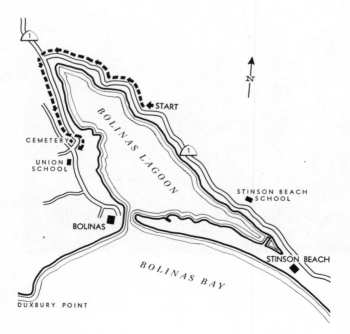

Around the Lagoon in Bolinas

■ The sleepy V-shaped lagoon called Bolinas may take its name from the Tamal Indian word for stormy, from the name of an Indian girl, from an Indian village, from the Spanish word for whale, "Boulinas," or from Francisco Bolanos, pilot of the Sebastian Vizcaino expedition of 1603. All four theories have their supporters.

In its time, it has also been called Rialto Cove. By whatever name, it lies at the southermost end of the Point Reyes peninsula in a classic rift valley of the San Andreas fault. As the great blue heron, which nests nearby, flies, it is about 12 miles north of San Francisco. As Highway 1 twines along the cliffs, it is more like 21. To the queasy, this can seem like 2100.

Like two children that have gone down to the sea to play, Bolinas village, originally Jugville, and Stinson Beach, once called Willow Camp, stand as casual sentinels on its opposing shores. Trailing in the water between them, barely torn by a channel, is a long curving scarf of fashionable sandspit recently christened Sea Drift.

Few places so close to the city are so enticing to walk as the border of Bolinas Lagoon. Here, on the one hand, are tide flats and shore wildlife that depends upon shallow water. On the other are cliffy tree-filled canyons plunging down from Bolinas Ridge to the water.

To enjoy some of both, begin this walk at McKinnon's Point, two miles north of Stinson Beach School. Between 1852 and 1870, the brothers Thomas and William Johnson built and launched schooners, among them the *Anna Caro-*

lina and the *Effi Newell,* registered at 80 tons, from this point. Under the Marin County master plan, this may once again become a boat launching point.

Walk north, skirting the shore and following the road. Watch the water for the green heron, the snowy egret and the black-crowned night heron, which feed in the lagoon. Two bigger birds, the great blue heron and the American egret, can often be seen flying to and from treetop rookeries of Audubon Canyon and the adjacent Garden Canyon. (Tours along the trail overlooking the rookeries may be arranged in advance by appointment with the Marin Audubon Society or the Golden Gate Audubon Society, P.O. Box 441, Tiburon.)

Try to imagine redwood trees "second only to the Big Trees of Calaveras" filling these canyons. Fifteen million feet of lumber, pilings, railroad ties, shingles and cordwood came out of the canyons near Bolinas in the 20 years following the Gold Rush. Much of it was lightered over the sand bar, then taken to San Francisco by sea, along with cargoes of potatoes and produce.

Hew to the shoreline when the road meets the Olema turnoff and swing west. Soon you will be abreast of a few pilings in the water, the remnants of a wharf once used by a double-ender passenger ship whose skipper was known only as Captain Town Meeting and later by *The Owl,* skippered by Captain Louis B. Petar.

As recently as 1912, Helen Bingham reported, in her book *In Tamal Land,* taking the Bolinas stage drawn by four horses from West Point on Mount Tamalpais to the Dipsea resort, in what is now Stinson Beach, and thence by steam schooner across the lagoon. The Flagstaff Inn, now gone, was her destination.

Thirty years earlier she might have met a man called The Blacksmith living in a cask on the beach, and another, Captain J. A. Morgan, living in the stranded forecastle of a ship. On one occasion the eccentric blacksmith, annoyed at finding no one in the village on his arrival, poured salt water in every well.

When you come abreast of the dump sign reading "Garden Cuttings and Prunings Only" peer in. This area is labeled as a park on Marin's master plan.

The unusual garage across the road is worth a stop to see, a few hundred yards further. It is the shop of Espinet, builder of fine furniture. Be sure to go behind, across the footbridge, to see the round showcase of museum pieces.

By the time the road reaches the cemetery junction, you will have walked the boundary of the lagoon acreage Marin planners hope to purchase for recreational purposes, and to insure for all time the feeding grounds of the rare birds that frequent it.

Bolinas' Wharf Road and Brighton Avenue form the center of this quiet country village.

14

Bolinas houses come down to the shore. Clammers who used to dig for cockles here are now warned away by water pollution signs.

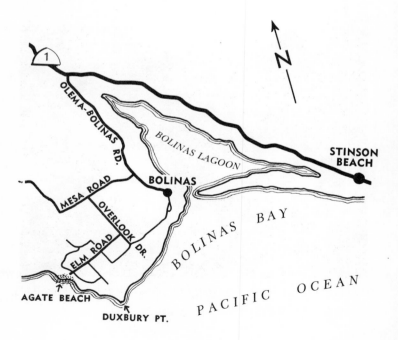

Bolinas Is too Good to Last

■ To step into Bolinas is to arrive, time out of mind, 50 years ago. Here in the country's heart, where the grass grows green, life is the same sweet life that it has always been. The pace is the rhythm of the tides. The modern world seems very far away from this western shore. There is one general store, an antique store, a bookstore, a laundromat, three establishments that call themselves respectively Snarley's, Scowley's and Smiley's, and surprisingly two excellent restaurants, Gibson House and Tarantino's.

Fog and a five-mile remove from Highway 1 have kept Bolinas pristine. For how much longer is anyone's guess. First time visitors usually say, "This is too good to last" after a first time around the Bolinas beach loop.

To make this walk, transport yourself to Bolinas, 22 miles north of San Francisco on the very edge of the land. You approach skirting Bolinas Lagoon, which conservationists have been fighting valiantly to keep free of motor boats and motels. The road swings away from the lagoon at Gospel Flat. In lumbering days, when the canyons near the lagoon supplied wood for San Francisco, the names of Bolinas satellite communities were more forthright, Dogtown, Jugtown and Greaserville.

The town proper is heralded by an excellent terminal vista that appears unexpectedly ahead on the road. This is the charming white Calvary Presbyterian Church, an historical landmark. In sight of it, park as soon as you find a place.

Facing the church, bear right along Brighton Avenue past the modest country-style cottages that could have stepped right out of the pages of Sinclair Lewis. At least one house is haunted by a sea captain's restless ghost. Vacationing San Franciscans are interlarded along Brighton with townspeople. All take their turns at the tennis courts across the street.

Soon the little street will reach the beach. Go down the ramp beside a large white house to the beach for a taste of the tangy Bolinas seaside flavor. Bear left along the sand. If it is low tide, one can walk around the cliff. Horses, dogs, sunners, swimmers, surfers, toddlers, fishermen, hippies and nuns, their habits billowing in the wind, make up the beach composite. The Roman Catholic sisters who come from different orders to a retreat here have made a colorful note in many a painting of the cliffy Bolinas shore.

Look north to locate Duxbury Reef, and far beyond it, Point Reyes. Suddenly as you are walking south, the long Sea Drift sandspit of Stinson Beach is visible, its houses snuggled down into the sand almost inconspicuously. In clear weather, the distant southern viewpoint is San Francisco with the white houses of the Richmond and Sunset districts flung across the City's slopes like laundry drying on the ground.

Go over near the channel to Bolinas Lagoon to see how narrow is the divide between this beach and Sea Drift. Strong swimmers crossing it may be carried 1000 feet off course by the stronger current.

Soon the beach ends at Wharf Road. Ascend to the street and walk along, past the waterside houses and houseboats. Across from the dock, the nearest white building, once a Coast Guard station, now houses the College of Marin marine biology station. It offers excellent ecological preservation walks on Duxbury Reef and Kent Island by pre-arrangement.

Bolinas Lagoon divides the relaxed and old-timey town of Bolinas and chic Sea Drift, a sandspit Pacific Heights in Stinson Beach.

15

Mt. Wittenburg is the highest landmark in the Point Reyes National Seashore. Part of Inverness Ridge, it lies just north of Park Headquarters in Olema.

View from Mount Wittenburg

■ "For pure, unadulterated sea air, full of fog and oxygen, charged with ozone, salubrious and salsuginous, invigorating and life-giving air, that will make the pulses leap and bring the roses to the cheek, one should go to Point Reyes, where it can be had at first hand, bereft of nothing."

So wrote H. P. Munro-Fraser in his authoritative *History of Marin County*, describing in 1880 the climate of what is now Point Reyes National Seashore.

The walker who makes the climb from Bear Valley to the bald crest of 1407-foot Mount Wittenburg, a southern highpoint of Inverness Ridge, in spring will find the sea air charged as well with the sweet scent of lupine, California poppies, cowslips and iris.

Pack a knapsack lunch and canteen, for there are no concessions within the seashore area. Make an information stop at the Bear Valley Ranger Station near the farmhouse that serves as park headquarters. This is about a mile from Olema, 35 miles northwest of San Francisco on Highway 1.

Park at the trailhead. At the outset walk south on Bear Valley Trail. Almost immediately Sky Trail to Mount Wittenburg takes off uphill on the left. Ignore it for the moment. Instead, continue on Bear Valley Trail to see the "butterfly tree," a great white eastern dogwood. Look for it across the creek. Watch along the trail for five-finger ferns which grow in profusion here. Soon Meadow Trail forks uphill on the right. Take it to make a gentle climb to the peak through a primeval forest of Douglas firs for which Inverness Ridge is noted.

After many long switchbacks through laurel, madrone, Bishop pines and the firs, the trail reaches a beautiful grassy meadow where the observant may sometimes spot a mountain beaver or a black-tailed deer. The trail, almost lost in deep grass, goes back into the trees at the far end of the meadow to cross Sky Trail soon thereafter on a bare lower shoulder of Mount Wittenburg. Follow Sky Trail right around a broad curve until a sign indicates the mountaintop and a bare single path winds uphill.

Mount Wittenburg was named for a man reputed to have had a ranch here. It may have been at the corral site visible in a little crotch of land below the peak toward the west. A cairn of rock on which a sign notes the elevation of the crest and another nearby supporting a red, much-faded rag of flag are all that mark the mountaintop.

On a foggy day, hiker Mark Kitchell says, "on the crest it is like living with gods on Mount Olympus or Parnassus. All you see are other mountaintops." On a fair day, the view is stupendous, with Olema looking like a toy railroad town and Drake's Estero like a map on the land.

Abbott's Lagoon, the boot-shaped lake that almost touches the sea at the great Point Reyes beach, is named for a hero, Carleton S. Abbott. In 1861 when the clipper ship *Sea Nymph* went ashore, a boatload of men and the captain trying to land in a small boat were capsized in the breakers. Abbott "grasped a long riata in his hand and plunged boldly into the crested breakers. With a skillful twirl of the rope in mid-air, he sent it with unerring aim over the captain's head, and in a trice had dragged him safely ashore. This was repeated until all the men were saved."

Look for Mount Tamalpais, Mount St. Helena and Mount Diablo to get your bearings. When you have gloried in the surroundings sufficiently, or finished your picnic lunch, pick up Sky Trail for a quick return. It winds, a single footpath, through lupine and poppies over the southeasterly side of the mounded crest.

From Mt. Wittenburg the walker looks down on Olema and ranches along Highway 1. Sir Francis Drake Highway loops east to San Rafael through rolling hills.

16

Trailhead parking in Bear Valley indicates the great popularity of the Point Reyes National Seashore in its undeveloped state. Conservationists fear that it will "become another Yosemite Valley" unless the motorcar is checked, like a coat, at the door.

Walk in the Woods to the Seashore

■ Beautiful Bear Valley, a natural break in Inverness Ridge at Point Reyes National Seashore, is 35 miles northwest of San Francisco by way of the weaving, winding, State Highway 1. From the City, it is an ideal, one-day excursion.

Seasoned hikers and park rangers refer to Bear Valley Trail as "an old ladies' stroll," because it is fairly level. At least one conservationist, fearful of threatened overdevelopment if the seashore is opened to private enterprise, also calls it "a Yosemite Valley of the future."

This it may become. Today it is unspoiled and to the casual walker not in gung-ho climbing condition, Bear Valley Trail will be pleasurable indeed. It rambles for 4.4 miles of ranch roadway along two singing creeks which drain in opposite directions, through Bishop pines, Douglas fir, madrones, laurels and horse-chestnut trees to the ocean. At the shore, cliffs, agate-strewn pocket beaches, blowholes, seastacks, little waterfalls, tidepools and wind-worn meadows reward the walker.

Begin this walk on the sunniest day possible. Coastal valleys are gloomy in the fog. Bring a light-weight lunch you can carry easily, and a canteen, for there are no concessionaires. (Nearest source of refreshments is in the little town of Olema.)

Stop first at the information booth at park headquarters, located at what was formerly the Bear Valley dairy ranch.

Architect Earl R. MacDonald, who did much of the work on the ranch during the 1930's, designed the bunkhouse that is now the ranger station. The milk station, he says, has become the park fire station. A dairy building stood where the information office is now located. Trail maps and bird count lists are distributed here free.

There are also postcards, U. S. Geological Survey maps, paperbound copies of *Island in Time*, Harold Gilliam's book on Point Reyes, and a charming book, *Exploring Tidal Life*, prepared by teachers and students under the National Science Foundation, for sale at the information building.

After a stop here, drive beyond additional ranch buildings to a trail-head parking lot and look for the seashore-blue sign marking the trail, near a white gate. Rules posted nearby indicate horses, bicycles and leashed dogs may also use the trail, but not cars.

Bear Valley has 40 miles of trail for hikers, many of them a spiderweb of unused ranch roads. More ambitious climbers and physical fitness nuts may want to follow Sky Trail west from this point up the 1407-foot elevation of Mount Wittenburg, then loop south to the coast and return via Bear Valley. Amblers should look for the road south.

At the outset, the road and you will be following Bear Valley Creek which drains in the opposite direction from Coast Creek thanks to the San Andreas fault on whose geologically tender edge this land lies.

Gradually the road rises with the land. After passing a meadow (with a few picnic tables) the road parallels Coast Creek. Stop occasionally and listen to the singing water. Each creek, and the little streamlets, springs and falls that join them, makes its own music, almost symphonic at the ocean.

The meadow has a past history as location of a hunt club which Presidents Taft and Teddy Roosevelt visited. At one time an excursion surrey made regular runs from Olema House to the beach via Bear Valley Road, at $1 per passenger.

Along the path are "the blue forget-me-nots that grow for happy lovers." Look also for birds. The Point Reyes peninsula has had the second-highest bird count in the nation.

After passing several subsidiary paths, Bear Valley Trail leaves the roadway in a meadow within sound of the sea. Walk out to the cliff viewpoint to reconnoiter, then follow the path south that says "Blowhole—Caution." Here is high adventure. At low tide, the trail gives access to the beach through a wave-carved arch. As the tide rises, one can see the ocean at work carving ever more seastacks.

If you come upon a little shard of Ming pottery on the beach, you can chalk it up to the leavings of either Sir Francis Drake's ship *Golden Hind* or Sebastian Cermeno's Spanish galleon *San Agustin*, if you care to. Agates are commoner.

Next time you come, plan to make it a spring wildflower trip, when the big dogwood tree near the start of the trail is in bloom. If you want to see where the earth swallowed the cow in the earthquake of 1906, try the shorter Earthquake Trail.

Visual prize for hikers to the ends of seashore trails may be a waterfall, a blow hole, a glimpse of migrating whales, great stretches of sandy beach, steep cliffs, seals sporting in the surf, or an infinity of sky and sea.

17 *Ten Mile Beach is the great remote stretch of the Pacific strand where comers ride ashore like Poseidon's stallions, sometimes carrying Japanese fishing floats with them.*

Thoreau's Kind of Walk

■ "My life is like a stroll upon the beach," wrote Henry David Thoreau. "As near the ocean's edge as I can go." To him, the ocean, and those who sailed it, were only a little deeper down upon the strand.

The great beach of Point Reyes National Seashore, 40 miles north of San Francisco, would have been Thoreau's kind of walk. Indeed, when October's bright blue weather arrives, it is a fine walk for anyone.

It is an infinity of galloping combers, mounting successively a fine clean swath of uninterrupted, uncrowded sand. It is an odd, waveworn chunk of weathered driftwood here, a random twisted branch there. Once in awhile, after a storm, there is one of those great treasures, a Japanese glass fishing float, with all its handblown, ingrown romance.

Locally known as Ten Mile Beach, the great Point Reyes beach may actually be 10, 11 or 12 miles long. Authorities differ. Whatever its length, weekend walkers, beachcombers, picnickers and fishermen who walk the beach now have a measure of their progress. It is three miles of beachwalking from the wayside exhibit and pavilion of Point Reyes Beach North to that of Point Reyes Beach South.

Either place is an excellent starting point, for there are privies and parking at both. If there is a stiff on-shore breeze, it is the better part of wisdom to begin at the southerly point so the wind will be at your back for the return trip.

Not long ago I made this walk with Sally and Peter Behr, a former Marin County Supervisor, who led the "Save Our Seashore" campaign. We parked at the north lot. It was raining. One of those late summer spitty fogs that seem mild enough until one discovers the hair is dripping, the face glistening and the sweater beaded with a million diamonds. The walk was exhilarating, despite the "liquid sunshine."

We examined the five portholes in the wayside exhibit for starters. The first is devoted to waves, rip currents and floating debris, the second to birds, the third to high and low tides, the fourth to a map of the area and the last to fish found near shore here. There are good illustrations of the red tail surfperch and of the silver surfperch.

Before we had walked half a mile, we examined the catch of a man from Napa who had caught five of one variety and seven of the other.

As we walked, Sally Behr recalled picnics she had had on the beach with her children. Peter recounted some of the history of the beach where 13 ships were wrecked between 1861, when the *Sea Nymph* went down, and 1924 when the waters claimed the *Tai Vin*.

Most famous among the Point Reyes beach wrecks was the *Warrior Queen*, wrecked in 1875. A local rancher, Henry Claussen, swam out in a storm with a line, only to find all boats, men and papers gone. Rather than try a landing in the dangerous surf, her crew put to sea and made San Francisco the next day. For years the *Warrior Queen* figurehead adorned the nearby ranch. Thirteen more ships were wrecked on the cliffs of Point Reyes despite the lighthouse (not open to the public) and at least three men from the life saving station were drowned while attempting rescues.

Twelve more ships have been claimed by Drakes Bay, among them the *Lurline*, in 1903. It was Drakes Bay that had the first recorded shipwreck on the California coast, that of the Spanish Galleon *San Agustin* in 1595.

Sir Francis Drake, who had arrived 16 years earlier, in 1579, was luckier.

There are 113 known sites of aboriginal villages, all with interesting kitchen middens, in the seashore area but the first vast landholder was Antonio Maria Osio, who also once owned Angel Island in San Francisco Bay. Exclusive of the villages of Inverness, Olema and Bolinas, all of which abut the National Seashore, there were 62 private owners of Point Reyes land in 1960 when seashore acquisition began.

Both Marin County and the State of California have made gifts of land to the National Seashore, the former the 52-acre Sir Francis Drake Beach and the latter 11,415 acres of tidelands.

When you reach a few outlying picnic tables, and a few more fishermen, you will have arrived at the other Point Reyes beach parking lot. If it is the south one, check the wayside exhibit for its panel on sea lions and stellar seals, then head back.

Cliffs at Ten Mile Beach have been a help to navigators for 300 years, as they can be seen from miles at sea.

18

Earthquake Walk follows the rift in Bear Valley which re-routed adjacent streams so that they flow in opposite directions. From this catwalk bridge one can touch the water.

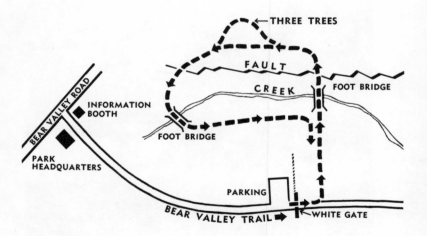

Where the Earthquakes Come From

■ "Probable nor'east to sou'west winds, varying to the southard and westard and eastard and points between; high and low barometer, sweeping round from place to place; probable areas of rain, snow, hail and drought, succeeded or preceded by earthquakes with thunder and lightning," wrote Mark Twain in a versatile all-purpose weather report.

It couldn't miss.

Neither can the man who predicts another quake along the San Andreas fault, the classic textbook example of a fault zone. Sooner or later the edgy earth will shake. Next scene: falling plaster. Followed by seers and prophets taking bows.

The ghosts of earthquakes past lie all about us on the fault. Bear Valley is one of the best places to see them. It is located in Point Reyes National Seashore, about 30 miles north of San Francisco near the point where the Sir Francis Drake Boulevard meets State Highway 1.

If you come along Highway 1 via Stinson Beach, you will pass sag ponds, eucalyptus tree offsets, fault traces of both the '06 and several earlier quakes, two quake-redirected streams lying within 1000 feet of each other, one of which empties into Tomales Bay and the other into Bolinas Lagoon, and other vestiges of earthquake activity. Look for them after you pass the Bolinas turn-off and before you reach Olema.

For a closer look on foot, the best earthquake evidence has been dramatized with a new Self-Guiding Earthquake Loop Trail through pleasant woodland near the farmlike headquarters of the National Seashore. It goes through terrain, like Olema Valley, that bears great scars of the 1906 shake, yet has grades gentle enough for toddlers or grandparents.

To enjoy this walk, park at the trailhead lot, planning to stop at park headquarters later. Trails for Bear Valley all start beyond a white gate at the far end of the lot (opposite side from picnic area and privies). About 50 feet beyond the white gate, look on the left for a sign and for two grass-grown auto tracks that take off into the meadow.

Follow these for a few hundred yards through waves of wild oats and other grasses rippling in the wind. Beyond the great old bay trees, one finds a big blue sign that announces, "The San Andreas fault separates Point Reyes from the mainland" and shows a topographic map that explains the "earth crack" along the Olema-Bolinas area you may just have traveled.

Nearby, just before you reach a bridge with handrails crossing Bear Valley Creek, is the next explanatory sign describing the earthquake activity which changed the direction of the creek so it no longer joins Olema Creek beyond the hill.

The next sign brings out the amusing, and possibly apocryphal, story of the cow that fell into the crack. Alan Galloway, in *Geology of Northern California*, issued by the State Division of Mines says, "At the . . . Shafter Place, a cow fell headfirst into a fault crevice," and quotes G. K. Gilbert, "The closure which immediately followed left only the tail visible." Park officials, however, have found no physical evidence.

Bear uphill to the left on an oaken slope. Soon you reach a short side loop trail that celebrates three majestic trees, a California bay or pepperwood, a tan oak and a live oak. The latter is overgrown with lichens and just out of danger range has a dangling poison oak ideally situated to demonstrate to children, and greenhorn walkers.

A tongue-in-cheek sign warns walkers to tread softly, lest

they set off another tremor. There is also another puzzle on this imaginative trail planned by ranger Jim Lyles. Rather than give it away, we will leave it to the walker to discover on one of the trail markers how granite landed in this unlikely spot.

Shortly one is walking on the fault line itself. Soon there is even more dramatic earthquake alteration in displaced trees and a fence line of posts crossing the fault line which demonstrates where the land moved 15 feet.

Follow the trail looping back, for the fun of crossing the stream again, this time on an intimate catwalk bridge so close to the water you can dip your fingers in.

On the Earthquake Trail walkers can see fence-posts offset 15 feet by the Quake of '06, plus other evidence of more recent quivers along the San Andreas Fault.

19

Tomales Bay is great for day sailors. A Loch Ness monster would probably find its water too shallow for comfort.

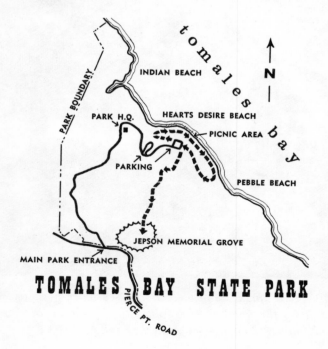

The Loch Ness of Marin

■ Whenever another of the outsized footprints of Bigfoot, the elusive monster of the North woods, is discovered and followed by attendant merriment, I find myself with an almost overwhelming urge to start a watery rumor. The rumor would be that something which looks like the Loch Ness monster had been sighted in Tomales Bay.

Loch Ness, like Tomales Bay, lies in a great long geological fault, which is also a firth connected to the sea. There is sufficient physical similarity of conformation that James Black, an early Marin County settler, named a western shore community for his birthplace, Inverness, in whose shire Loch Ness lies.

So far, my conscience has kept this irresponsible urge in check (if a Scot's conscience does not keep her from sinning, my Grandfather Watson used to warn, it will surely keep her from enjoying it). Nevertheless, I keep hoping that some enterprising junk-sculptor will nail four monstrous old half-track tires to a raft and set it afloat some misty night.

I suspect it is this, as much as the Bishop pines and the cockles, that brings me back every so often for a walk in Tomales Bay State Park, four miles north of Inverness. As local residents know, it is a good walk for the National Seashore visitor who finds himself on Point Reyes on one of those gray days when the fog seems to have a cold edge that cuts to the bone.

If there is warmth and sheltered waterside walking to be had on the long peninsula on such a day, it is to be found in the sandy little coves and western shore beaches of Tomales Bay State Park.

Begin this walk with a stop at your local bait shop for a clam digging license. Bring your picnic and thermos (the nearest concessions are at Inverness), pay the 50-cent day use fee, park as near to the water as you can and you are then ready to explore this unspoiled 1018 acres of scenic excellence on foot.

The big parking area is at Heart's Desire Beach, with two other beaches in easy walking distance. Three-quarters of a mile north is Indian Beach. About one third of a mile south is Pebble Beach.

There are good trails through the woods overlooking the shore which take off from the parking circle, but if it is low tide, stick to the beach instead and join in or watch the carnival of clammers as they scrabble through the rocks for the succulent prize, *Paphia staminea*, also known as the rock cockle, the little-neck clam, hard shell clam, Tomales Bay cockle, rock clam or the ribbed carpet shell. Fifty is the limit and they must each be more than 1½ inches long.

Long before either Juan Rodriguez Cabrillo or Sir Francis Drake sailed past the Marin coast, Indians clawed among the rocks of this shore for clams much as people do today. Their name for the water which had filled the San Andreas rift zone was Lake Olemas. Since Tomales means "bay," today we are using a redundant name for this long narrow inlet. As you walk watch for redwinged blackbirds, tule wrens, Wilson snipe, clapper rails, bitterns and the beach front clowns—the sandpipers. Herons, ruddy ducks, scoters, grebes, willets and curlews are not uncommon.

Sometimes the great Point Reyes ravens pass overhead. Keep your eye peeled among the rocks and you may stumble on a shell of the little rare native oyster. Fences visible in some parts of Tomales Bay protect imported oyster beds from underwater predators.

When you have explored the beach, return to the parking circle to pick up Jepson Trail, named in honor of the late Willis Linn Jepson, a pioneer conservationist and founder of the School of Forestry at the University of California.

From the south side of the circle, the trail leads uphill through California laurel, madrone, oak and wax myrtle to a splendid stand of Bishop pine, the Jepson Memorial Grove. The Bishop pine, whose cones may hang on to the stem they encircle for 15 years, has built-in protection from forest fires. Its cones only open and seeds germinate after exposure to fire.

Take a last look at the bay before you leave. Something that looks like a Loch Ness monster may be lurking in the distance.

Tomales Bay often has sun when the rest of Point Reyes National Seashore is fogged in. And at Indian Beach there is a pocket of sand that is warm and sheltered all the time.

20

Nicasio has the same bucolic unspoiled dairyland that characterized all of Marin County a scant twenty years ago.

Marin's Quiet Country Village

■ Nicasio, a lovely little Marin town, is as unspoiled as the virtuous heroine in a 19th century melodrama. And like the melodrama there is a villain, probably a developer, lurking just over the hill. If he doesn't have designs on Nicasio's virgin landscape, it's only because he hasn't seen her yet.

To put it in the planner's way, Nicasio Valley has such "fragile environmental quality" one misplaced building or signpost could throw the entire ecology out of whack. Even a small tract in Nicasio's little valley could create a smog basin.

Fortunately there is a hero, riding to the rescue of this fair village—well before it is in distress. It is a research team jointly sponsored by the Marin County Planning Department and America the Beautiful Fund with the cooperation of the Nicasio Property Owners Association. They have come up with a land-use program to keep Nicasio livable.

To see what an unspoiled countryside looks like, as much of Marin County looked a scant 20 years ago, why not come for a walk around Nicasio's central plaza. Take the Lucas Valley Road just north of San Rafael. It meanders through bucolic countryside for 10 beautiful undeveloped miles. Then suddenly one is detouring at sharp right angles beside what seems to be a field in the heart of a minuscule village. Park where you can, preferably in front of Rancho Nicasio.

This was the site of the first house built here in 1852 by Noah Corey, who finished his home with shakes sawn with a circular saw driven by horsepower. The second building to stand on the site was the three-story Hotel Nicasio, an effort of William G. Miller, built in 1867, and the center of Nicasio's social life until it burned in 1940. Glenn Kerch, Nick Kobseff and Dorothy Mead are the proprietors of the Rancho Nicasio, its general store, post office, restaurant and swimming pool.

Notice the baseball field and bleachers in the corner of the central square whose nicely carved sign says George Bill Till Road.

Earliest recorded history of the square indicates that it was proposed as a site for a courthouse in the 1860s at a time when Nicasio had a population of 600, two nearby lumber mills, and yearned to be the county seat.

It may, however, actually have been in use as a plaza as early as 1835 when Governor Figueroa granted the surrounding 20 square leagues of land to Teodosio Quilajeaqui and others of his tribe, a claim later rejected by the Yankee Land Commission of 1855. "Before the Gringo came," California laws, in some respects more enlightened than our own, required a certain percentage of land for common public use. The "Nicasio" Indians, actually Coastal Miwoks, like the town, take their name from a convert chief whose name saint was Nicasius.

Walk westerly toward the San Geronimo Road. At the corner, look north to see a village street where a Californian Huck Finn or Tom Sawyer would feel at home. Then turn south, following the square past the Druid Hall. A butcher shop, a grocery and a blacksmithy, whose first smith, Thomas Ward, set up his forge and anvil outdoors under a spreading oak tree, have been fixtures along this rural way in the past.

At the next corner walk east, toward the charming white church, Our Lady of Loretto, which celebrated its centenary in 1965. About abreast of the rose-covered trellis en route, pause to look up in the hills at wind-sculptured trees. Planner Al Solnit says Nicasio Valley's flat center bowl was totally filled by stream erosion from the surrounding mountains. Landslides are common in this unstable area.

Recent visitors to Nicasio can remember two buffalo (since deceased) that grazed in the pasture behind the church. Turn north at Mary Evelyn Lane and complete the square. If one comes along this way on a weekday, sometimes the only sound is the singing of wind in the trees.

Finish this walk inside Rancho Nicasio for a look at the large mural whose central figure is Jose Calistro, last chief of the Nicasio Indians. A mounted buffalo head hangs nearby.

Either one would have appreciated Marin County poet Lew Welch's moving words, "This is the last place, there is nowhere else to go . . . at the feet of the final cliffs of all Man's wanderings."

Nicasio's one-room school is now a private home and the schoolhouse is a few hundred yards north along San Geronimo Road. The owner has carefully preserved the school qualities.

21

Wolf House built by Jack London was gutted by fire before he could ever move in.

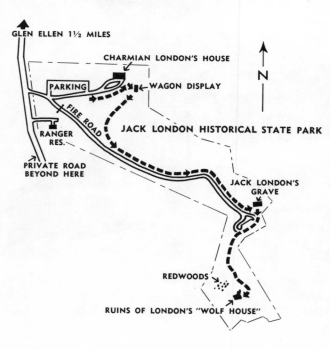

GLEN ELLEN 1½ MILES

CHARMIAN LONDON'S HOUSE

PARKING

WAGON DISPLAY

N

FIRE ROAD

RANGER RES.

JACK LONDON HISTORICAL STATE PARK

PRIVATE ROAD BEYOND HERE

JACK LONDON'S GRAVE

REDWOODS

RUINS OF LONDON'S "WOLF HOUSE"

Where Jack London Used to Walk

■ "I would rather be a superb meteor, every atom of me in magnificent glow, than a sleepy and permanent planet," wrote San Francisco-born Jack London, the spectacular literary figure, immediately preceding World War I.

He meant it. In a lifetime that ended at the age of 40 in 1916, Jack London had managed to be a newsboy, cannery hand, "boy socialist," oyster pirate, tramp, gold prospector, war correspondent, world traveler and to write 50 or so books, most of them wildly successful. Since history refuses to let sleeping prose lie, one day he may well be rediscovered as California's greatest native storyteller.

When it happens, scholars will beat a path to the little Sonoma Valley town of Glen Ellen, about 50 miles north of San Francisco off Highway 12 between Sonoma and Santa Rosa. Here, a mile out of town on the Jack London Ranch Road, 40 acres of his beloved, vast "Beauty Ranch" overlooking the Valley of the Moon have been since 1959 the Jack London Historical State Park.

Since this is a park from which the automobile is excluded, it has special pleasures for walkers, including a museum, a display of early farm implements in their natural location, a pioneer cemetery, Jack London's grave and two romantic dream houses. In the great classic continental tradition, one of them, the picturesque romantic ruin of Wolf House, is the destination for the principal woodland trail.

To see for yourself, begin this walk in the parking lot at the entrance of the park. A good map is displayed near the trail entrance at the east end of the lot. After orienting yourself, walk up the short rise about 500 yards to "The House of Happy Walls," which was the home of London's second wife, Charmian, between 1919 and 1955.

It is now a museum dedicated to the man who liked to be called "Wolf," admission 25 cents. If you arrive in the late afternoon, save this visit as the capper for your walk. A chain goes across the trailhead at 4 p.m.

Pick up the trail to Wolf House east of the museum. Within another 100 yards, beside a beautiful toyon tree, one comes upon the wagon display, provided, like the acreage itself, through the generosity of London's nephew Irving Shepard, heir to the property. When you have examined the old implements, follow the trail downhill.

Soon you will reach a stream and a fire road. Bear left at the road and take it through woodland until you reach a clearing and a bench. Jack London's grave and that of two children of old-time settlers are a few hundred feet off the trail on the knoll uphill on the left, a short and interesting digression.

Inspect it if you have time, then bear right to reach the redwood grove in which Wolf House, a melancholy skeleton all arches and towers, is located. As Dr. Franklin Walker, professor of English at Mills College, has described it in the 1967 Keepsake Series of the Book Club of California, "Wolf House was planned as a vernacular artifact; maroon volcanic boulders were surmounted by balconies of unpeeled redwood trunks and open handhewn rafters. Local blue slate and cobblestones went into the half-dozen fireplaces and the several exterior staircases . . . .

"Some 80 feet square and three stories high . . . it featured a large workroom, isolated from the rest of the house, with a library beneath it reached by a circular staircase. It contained many guest rooms and a living room which rose for two stories, with a fireplace big enough to roast an ox; this hospitality center was roomy enough to house Charmian's Steinway in an alcove and to seat 50 people for a banquet.

Downstairs was a big play room, for men only; above it was a large outdoor pool to be stocked with mountain bass."

Fire destroyed Wolf House August 22, 1913, just before the Londons were to move in. The furniture and collections went instead into "The House of Happy Walls" where the walker can see them in the museum until 5 p.m.

If you plan to make it a day-long outing, carry your lunch in your pocket, for the park has no tables or other formal facilities for picnicking, but there is no objection to dining "Jack London style" on a stump or bench. A leisurely walk to Wolf House and back will take about an hour and 15 minutes.

Irving Sheppard, pointing at a picture of his uncle, Jack London, donated 15 of the park's 40 acres including Mrs. London's home; the ruins of Wolf House; the author's grave and his memorabilia to the state park system.

22

Admission to Fort Ross Chapel is free. Reconstructed after the 1906 Earthquake, the architecture duplicates exactly the 1828 original.

FORT ROSS

JENNER

RUSSIAN RIVER

SEBASTOPOL

SANTA ROSA

COTATI

PETALUMA

PACIFIC OCEAN

N

1

101

SAN FRANCISCO

A Walk for Escapists

■ One of the unique walks of the nine Bay Area counties is around Fort Ross, a remnant of Imperial Russia's one-time foothold in California.

For years it has come as a delightful shock to first-time venturers making their way along wonderful Highway 1 about 12 miles north of Jenner-by-the-Sea to sight the odd blockhouses and two-towered Russian Orthodox chapel silhouetted against the sky. Soon the reason for the Monroe Doctrine becomes clear. History slaps abruptly when one suddenly arrives within the wooden palisade of the fort.

If you yearn for escape from the commercialism of the holiday season, when the whales are migrating is the best of times to make this sea-coastal walk. Pack a picnic lunch. Gather up your children, spouse or friend, a duffel-coat and comfortable flat-heeled shoes.

Transport yourself via Highway 101 to Cotati or Santa Rosa, then cut west to Jenner on Highway 12, the road that rambles beside the Russian River, long a favorite with steelhead fishermen. To the Russians, this river was the Slavianka. Early Spaniards called it the San Sebastian.

The three acres on which Fort Ross stands have been a State Historical Monument since 1906 and admission is free. Since 1962, when the state purchased another 356 acres of land from the pioneer G. W. Call family, a natural seaside park has surrounded the stockade. There is a 50-cent fee for use of the new park and picnic area.

At the outset, park your car and walk over to the nearest eight-sided blockhouse. Its original counterpart was built in

1812 at the direction of Ivan A. Kuskoff, commander of the Russian-American Fur Company, who leased this land from the resident Pomo Indians for three blankets, three pair of breeches, three horses, two axes and some beads. Pomos from the nearby village of Mad Shi Nui were soon employed as otter hunters to supplement the Aleuts who had come with Kuskoff from Alaska. Within two years they exported 200,000 otter pelts.

The only known Battle of Fort Ross took place in 1844 after the Russians had left. It was a humorous seige in which armed white men approached to "run the Indians out of the fort." After evacuating their families, Indian braves held off the attackers with cannon and muskets, then at midnight slipped into the hills. The self-righteous attackers captured an empty fort, to which the Pomos returned after they left.

Locate the seaward sally port abreast of the stone monument which summarizes Fort Ross's subsequent history. Go through it, beyond the privies to the fence line for a look at the sea meadow and the sloping cliff.

Four ships were built at the boat landing that once stood below. San Francisco's Sacramento Street took its name from one of them, renamed, which anchored at its foot. Look across the creek for ruins of a tannery.

Return to the stockade for an inspection of Fort Ross Chapel, the charmer of this expedition. Unlike most Orthodox churches, this one never had a saint's name. It was restored after earthquake damage in 1906 tumbled the 1828 original. The front six-sided tower housed three bells, one of which is now in the museum collection. The rear dome sits on a round drum, which in turn surmonts the octagonal chapel. Originally it had 16 matched, naturally bent limbs from madrone trees as rafters. Services are conducted here on Russian Easter, Memorial Day and July 4.

Cross the highway to visit the Commander's house, now a museum. It was here that the journalist Alexander Rotcheff, last commandant of Ross, brought his young wife, the

Princess Helena Gagarin, with whom he had eloped from St. Petersburg. In 1841, the French traveller, Duflot du Mofras, described their choice library, French wines, pianoforte, gardens and glass house. Back of Ross on the mountain side were 700 horses, 800 cattle, 400 fruit trees and "a vineyard of 700 stocks, all of which were in good bearing condition."

Some of the fur hunters did not return to Sitka after John Sutter bought the property. One of them was the Finnish Captain Gustave Nybom who established the Inglenook Winery.

If the excellent museum exhibit of the sea otter makes you yearn to get down to the water, continue this walk south of the Russian River along any of the ten miles of beaches which make up the Sonoma Coast State Park.

Try to imagine little bidarkas, or kayaks, afloat in the surf, in which one hunter would hold a screaming baby otter captive while his companion harpooned the parents that came to the rescue. This is how they decimated the herds which only now are becoming re-established.

At $700 a pelt, even a Czar felt otters were fair game. The Czar was the president of the Russian-American Fur Company.

23 *Salt Point is probably the most beautiful spot on the North Coast.*

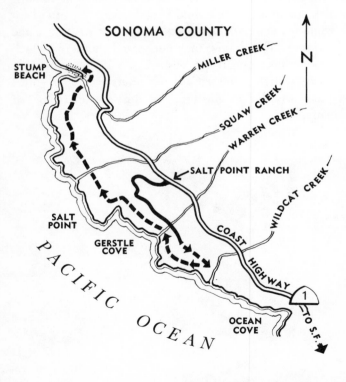

A Winter Walk on the Coast

■ For stimulating walking on a winter morning, few places can match Salt Point, the southern section of old El Rancho German on the beautiful Sonoma coast.

Here a dozen little coves and inlets, each more unusual than the last, are set about by sea stacks, natural bridges, caves, tide pools, underwater paths, rocky bluffs, long meadows, small forests, a beach and the estuaries of four creeks conceived as an educational as well as recreational facility by both the State Park system and Sonoma County educators. It is a shoreline so ecologically rich it has become a living laboratory for school camping.

To explore it yourself, head north on State Highway 1. Turn west off the highway about seven miles past Fort Ross at the big fish sign of Salt Point Ranch, whose owners presently charge visitors $1.50 per car for "trespass camping" or day use. Pay up at the ranch house, once part of a Salt Point hotel, and follow the ranch road down to the shore, as far south as you can drive. You will then be at Gerstle Cove, a favorite with scuba divers. Park, walk south, crossing Warren Creek to see wave-cut bluffs that look like great eroded bones, brains or tiki gods. Others, student Frank Kortum said, as he conducted us on this walk, "look like great dinosaurs waiting to come alive at some future date."

When you have clambered about the enticing waterworn crevices as far as Wildcat Creek, turn back. This approximates at the shore the southern boundary of Rancho German, granted by Mexican Governor Pio Pico to Captain

Ernest Rufus in 1846. It is also the waterfront perimeter of the 3000 acres in Salt Point Ranch. Agriculturally, this land is so lean it has been estimated it will only support 200 sheep.

In Indian days it may well have supported twice that many Pomos, the talented basketweavers who lived here on acorns, elk, fish, seaweed, and, in a pinch, roasted grasshoppers. Pomos still live nearby at a rancheria inland from Stewart's Point.

There are 3.7 miles of shoreline included in what will soon be Salt Point Educational Park. Fifteen camping areas, many of them east of Highway 1, are envisioned, but more important, certain of the coves will be sealed off for five-year periods to re-establish the normal balance of natural life.

Until they were denuded by the Aleut hunters brought to nearby Fort Ross by the Russian American Fur Company, these rocks were frequented by great herds of pelagic seals and sea otters. As you walk north, try to envision their bidarkas, or sea-going kayaks, bouncing on these dangerous waters. Whalers, too, have plied this coast, setting up their flensers and trypots on the shore.

Little lumber schooners of the "Scandinavian Navy" dodged in and out of the little dogholes here to load not only redwood, logged nearby, but great square building blocks, quarried for San Francisco. Notice the area near Salt Point itself still has many discarded building blocks, lying lichen-softened, on the ground. William Benitz, one of John Sutter's friends, was the quarry-master.

Highwaymen, stagecoach robbers, bull-teamsters, woodsmen, railroadmen, fishermen and rumrunners have all pitted themselves against the deep gorges of Salt Point at one time or another. Like the walker, they must have been relieved to reach smooth sandy Stump Beach at the mouth of Miller Creek, named not for the big redwood stump there, but for D. Stump, an early Salt Point township sheriff.

If your legs are still stout enough, go down the old farm road to the beach and look along the lower cliffs on the north side for fossil shellfish. Bullpine Camp, named for the Scotch pines planted along this coast 60 years ago by W. P. Frick, is at the north edge of Salt Point Ranch.

Stop here for directions to the redwood grove and the rhododendrons if you come in the blooming season. According to Bruce Walker, whose family has owned Salt Point Ranch for three generations, the native rhododendrons are every bit as lush as those at nearby Kruse State Preserve.

Sheltered coves and beaches add to the charm of Salt Point.

24

Vines ramble over these St. Helena aging rooms at Christian Brothers champagne cellar. Six other wineries are in walking distance along St. Helena's main street.

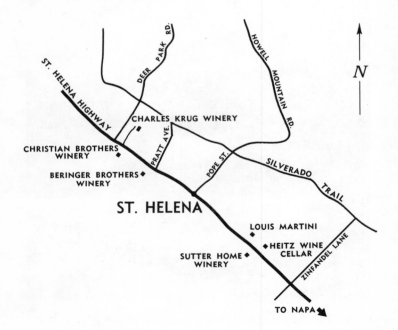

Of Wines and Vines in St. Helena

■ There are many good vineyard walks, all beautiful in spring or at the harvest season, when fruit hangs heavy on the vines and its bouquet puts an edge on the air.

During Wine Week, held as the grape-crushing comes to an end, the wineries are especially festive. My choice is St. Helena, where it is possible to visit six wineries in one day, all within walking distance of one another, passing through the remarkable Avenue of Elms en route.

Begin this walk at the venerable Charles Krug Winery at the northern edge of St. Helena, whose main street is also Highways 29 and 128. Here, on what was part of the Carne Humana land grant to his father-in-law, Dr. Edward Turner Bale (builder of the grist mill which still stands a few miles down the road), Charles Krug, a pioneer newspaper editor and first commercial vintner in the area, planted vines in 1861.

He had purchased them from his friend and former employer, Agoston Haraszthy, father of California viticulture. Notice the fine valley oak trees which shade the chateau and grounds. One, near what was Krug's horse and carriage barn and is now a rackhouse, is reputed to be 240 years old. Now owned by the Mondavi family, Krug winery employs 12 men to conduct tours, with a tour going out about every 20 minutes. Pullman Car No. 2979 standing in the vineyard is an auxiliary wine-tasting room.

From Krug, walk back to the highway through the vineyards and cross to the walk which borders Christian Brothers Wine and Champagne Cellars. Follow the handsome stone wall south until it is interrupted by the grotto-like arch that marks the winery entrance. Observe the handsome stonework on the old winery as you approach it. This is reputed to be the largest stone winery building in the world. It was built in 1888 as a co-operative venture, philosophically about 50 years ahead of its time. With this and other wineries, the Christian Brothers, a teaching order, support several schools, St. Mary's College among them.

Vineyard number three is Beringer. Return to the stone arch and walk south. This will lead through the impressive arch of irreplaceable old elms jeopardized like so many of our treasures by a projected freeway. Savor this shady avenue while you may.

Near the end of the lane of trees is the entrance to Beringer Brothers, Inc., renowned for the underground tunnels cut long ago by Chinese laborers and still in use for aging wine. William Mooser, architect of the Ghirardelli building, designed the interesting old house, now used for offices and wine-tasting. Beringer is still in the hands of the family who first planted here in 1876.

Bordering the road beside the winery buildings behind the house is a line of oleanders trained as trees, most of them greater than the average San Francisco street tree, and almost unbelievable for their variation of reds and pinks while in bloom.

When this fine old estate has revealed its charm, continue south again. In a short time you will be in the center of town, where there is a quaint little park behind the municipal buildings in which to rest or picnic. If you are still game for more wineries, follow Route 29 to the south edge of town to see Louis Martini, Sutter Home Winery, Heitz Wine Cellar, and Mondavi Winery.

At St. Helena, the Christian Brothers Winery overlooks the vineyards along "winery way", Highway 29. This great old stone building helps support the Christian Brothers school and colleges.

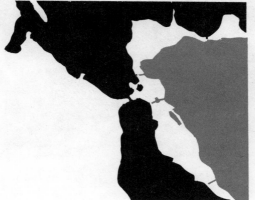

East Bay

25

Mortar Rock offers a shady nook from which one can enjoy a delightful view of the Bay.

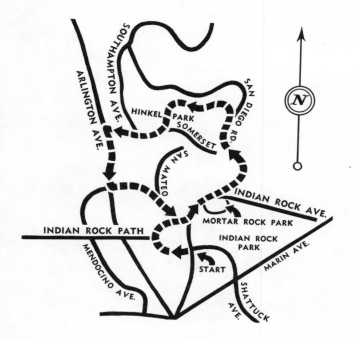

Bring Your Own Magic

■ Not long ago a poet at play took me for a walk through North Berkeley, a loop about two miles long, encompassing Indian Rock, Mortar Rock and John Hinkel Parks. En route we played a walking game in which landmarks and streets can be anything their appearance suggests. This had the effect of taking us through the higher altitudes of a country of our own construction.

Unless one has seen it in the rainy season, with torrents of water rushing down, it would not occur to most people to think of Marin Avenue as a rapids. But so it becomes in David Bromige's walking game. He also sees Oxford Street as a trail and San Diego Road as Happy Valley, which lies above an allied realm called, of course, Unhappy Valley.

The key to this walk lies in leaving your preconceived notions behind and really looking at what is about you. Begin this walk, as we did, where Shattuck Avenue meets Indian Rock Avenue, about a block uphill from The Circle, a convenient stop on the Number 7 bus.

Walk uphill to Indian Rock, the huge irregular rock mass looming overhead, climb it via the rear steps, then sit awhile on its eminence.

Imagination can make this a very tall mountain (at least 17,000 feet high) inspired by the knapsack and ropes clinging to an outcrop which are often used here by Sierra Club rock-climbing classes. "It's an allegory," David said. "See the climbers below struggling up one face when they could easily be walking up the steps on the other two sides."

From the peak, the little hill in Albany below seems to

be a closer echo of Mount Tamalpais in the distance. "The cloud of fog under the Golden Gate Bridge looks like cars could be sucked into it," Sherril Jaffe, a member of our caravan, suggested.

Go down the southern steps, then bear left, or east, to find a siren and two tall metal posts in a grove of eucalyptus. If you have a small child along, he will have no trouble imagining a magic forest.

About 300 feet downhill on the right is the entrance to Indian Rock Path. Enter it and loop the rock base, ignoring the straight segment that goes west. (It drops four blocks to Solano Avenue.)

Soon you will come out in a grove of leptospermum that could be, if you like, dinosaur trees guarding a rocky hobbit grotto.

Go up the stone steps past two stumps, emerging on San Mateo Avenue. Cross it, go uphill on Indian Rock Avenue and there, mid-block at the bend, is Mortar Rock Public Park.

For another spectacular view, climb the steps, bear right, then left around to the top. Here, sitting secluded in a ring of trees enhanced by natural bonsai growing from crevices in the rock, the great bay vista becomes a dramatic backdrop for the interplay of fog. Hurry down, for the steps, David likes to imagine, are only there one minute every year. Two hundred years ago, you might have surprised a hive of Indian women grinding pinole in the mortars that give this ornamental vest pocket park its name. If you use your imagination you might see them even today.

Then cross Indian Rock Avenue to come out opposite San Diego Road. Take it to a lower altitude. After passing an abandoned yard with a wall that looks Roman and a prickly pear that could be Aztec, look across from 801 San Diego for steps that lead down into Hinkel Park.

Turn right at the first landing to find a great view bench. Then look down the cliff to see Hinkel Amphitheater, where anything your imagination suggests can be on stage. The Floating Lotus Magic Opera has often been performed here.

Clinging to the cliffs, pass the hollow tree to reach a musical creek. Look both uphill and down, then continue through the woods to reach the park chalet. Continue downward through the oaks to find swings and teeter-totters. Walk to the left to descend through the amphitheater to its stage.

Veer toward the picnic tables for a fast loop back to Indian Rock via Somerset to Southhampton, then left at Arlington to Mendocino Path. Take Mendocino Path uphill. On the way, you will see a toucan and some racing pigeons in the Japanese garden aviary on the left, and a bigfoot print in the path. At San Mateo Avenue, bear right to return to Indian Rock. First one to the cave can be the hermit.

Indian Rock, in the residential heart of Berkeley, has steps carved on two faces. A steep cliff where Sierra Club mountaineer classes can practice rope work is on another.

26

Wildcat Peak looms over the sheltered Wildcat Valley, where a hidden rock has an imprint of a hand and the date 1815 inscribed on it.

Hunt for an Indian at Wildcat Peak

■ Somewhere, chiseled in low relief into a sandstone scarp on the southwest face of Contra Costa County's Wildcat Peak, there is probably the imprint of a hand, possibly an Indian hand, and the date "1810." Unless wind and rain have had their way with it, there is no reason to believe the hand isn't still there to be rediscovered above Wildcat fault by any bright-eyed, adventuresome climber.

No one has reported seeing it for the last ten years, however—either to the resident naturalist aide, Margery Hutchison of the Charles Lee Tilden Regional Park in which Wildcat Peak is situated, or to Carolyn Thatcher of the East Bay Regional Park District, who went out to see it, admittedly in an excited state of disbelief, the last time the hand was found.

Both of these young women, and the park system itself, would like to rediscover the Indian hand. To find it, of course, one must explore the terrain of Wildcat Peak and this in itself is a pleasant adventure, rewarded by a stupendous view from the crest or possibly a glimpse of a grey fox or a coyote.

The walk proper begins in Indian Camp for those who arrive by car. For those who come by public transportation, it begins at the junction of Grizzly Peak Boulevard, Wildcat Canyon Road, Spruce Street and Canyon Drive. The handsome new Shepherd of the Hills Lutheran Church is a good landmark. Indian Camp (now a picnic area but once used by the Costanoan Indians in their shell trade) is about two-tenths of a mile downhill on Canyon Drive.

Swing left at the tennis courts to find, beyond great weeping red gum trees, a gate which says "Only Foot Traffic." Wildcat Creek will be on your right, Jewel Lake on your left. The lake itself, surrounded by 700 acres in which no vehicles or picnickers are permitted, is hidden in blackberry shrubs and willows.

Follow the Jewel Lake service road, passing Jewel Lake Meadow and its watering trough, until you reach a rustic wooden bridge at the dam and spillway of Wildcat Creek. This is a good place to pause for a look at the lake, to listen for the phalarope, or spy the baby coots and baby ducks to be found here in June.

Wildcat Peak Trail, marked by the sign of a green mountain on a brown stake, takes up across the road from the bridge. It is a steep trail which reaches the Rotary Club International Peace Monument at its crest and the nearby Peace Grove of young redwood trees in about 45 minutes of open-country climbing. A loop following the peak trail up and a fire road and service road down circles the area in which the Indian hand is known to be located. Old Indian Trail, itself, lies within this circle but, thanks partly to the Wildcat Fault, it is a more rugged climb.

The Indian trail mounts through coast live oaks (and some poison oak) and under a chain of these anomalous scenery-defacing power line towers which I think of as Gecos. Geco is a word once shared with me by writer Graydon Walker, who says it derives from the initials for gas and electric company oaf. An oaf is a changeling. In the otherwise uncluttered country, my mind is stuck with Graydon's word, as the country itself is stuck with Gecos marching like militant Martian invaders.

There are several bare sandstone slabs from the old underlying Pliocene seaway for the climber to scramble over before he reaches the semicircular stone monument. Any of them is a good place to rest and observe the emerging panorama. Finally the bay is revealed, from the San Francisco Airport to Novato. Near at hand are Kensington School, a surplus missile site and an old quarry.

To the east, the unspoiled watershed of San Pablo Dam and its reservoir lie beyond the young sequoia grove at one's feet, where there are markers to Adlai Stevenson and John Foster Dulles, among others. Mount Diablo stands majestic in the distance and sometimes you can have a hawk's eye view of the red-tailed hawks circling below.

Wildcat Peak seen through the starkly architectural points of an old agave plant. High tension wires mar the otherwise unspoiled land.

27 *Tilden Park's Tewee Lake is wonderful for rainy day walking or duck watching.*

A Walk for a Rainy Day

■ For many people, the idea of walking in the rain conjures up some dismal visions. Serfs slogging through the steppes. Refugees fleeing a bombed city. An odd man out, collar up, pipe down on a wet slummy street.

Yet if you are dressed for it, rain walking can be very satisfying. The Japanese, who have made an art of sensual appreciation, take special rain walks to enjoy the sound on an umbrella, the bejewelling of moss, the splatter of droplets on a still pond.

In the Bay Area there are many places that rain gives a special quality. One of these is Jewel Lake in Tilden Regional Park, Berkeley. "Rain or shine" says the self-guiding nature trail booklet posted on the gate box, "there is always something to see and enjoy on the Jewel Lake Trail."

To make this walk, transport yourself to the north end of the park. Go in near the Kensington City Limits where Canyon Drive, Spruce Street, Grizzly Park and Wildcat Canyon Road merge. Take Canyon Drive down hill, turn left at the foot, away from the pony rides, drive as far as you can and park. If it's raining, be sure you have boots, rubbers, a poncho or other satisfactory rain gear. Pick up a trail booklet in the box by the gate, then walk uphill toward the attractive Little Farm, whose windmill, white fences, red barn, museum of old farm equipment and live animals, complete with noises, are easily discernible past the trees beyond the construction camp. Another box of trail guides to borrow is posted on the office gate, across the green lawn from the Little Farm. If empty, don't be discouraged; the 30 duck symbol trail markers are so well spaced, the trail is easy, even without the guide.

It is one mile long, has gentle grades and takes about an hour, depending on how long you linger.

Look for the path of chipped brush in front of the office, take it uphill, across the path to the nature lodge and a service road. You will arrive at a junction of many trails. The Jewel Lake duck marker indicates the downhill route which soon arrives at a plank bridge over the rivulet in Wildcat fault. Trail post number 1 is on the 100-foot-deep fault. Stand on the planks to see if you can feel earth tremors on it.

Then cross the second bridge, this one with a handrail, over Laurel Creek. Post 2 suggests looking overhead for redtailed hawks. Bear left up the steps to reach a grove of Coast live oak trees, Post 3. On the roadbed shelf above Post 4, the mushrooming is often good after a rain. Watch for poison oak downhill, however.

The eucalyptus grove, with its special pungency and silver blue leaves, almost seems like a conversational party in the rain. Beyond the bench, bear left on the main trail. Ducks quacking in the distance herald Jewel Lake. Sure enough, in a moment you are crossing the service road paralleling a feeder stream.

The next four trail posts point out blackberry, ninebark, willow and horsetail rush. Then you reach the raccoon pool. The trail goes under a low willow, over another, and Post 12, marking hedges, is often up to its neck in water during the rains, sometimes with little boys testing their rubber boots alongside.

Bear right, away from the stream through the pine trees, to Post 13, out near the road to reach the path and the alder trees, which love a damp shore. Post 15 is the half mile mark. It is also a natural viewing place for man-made Jewel Lake, built originally to serve as auxiliary water supply for Berkeley. In wet weather, the song of water through its sluice is fun to watch from the large footbridge over the spillway.

116

Go along the dam ridge, past coast redwoods, Douglas fir, California wax myrtle and cattails. As you continue on the point-to-point trail, watch for a large packrat's nest about 30 feet behind Post 25 and for the family of fox squirrels that live in an oak grove up the railroad tie steps.

As scenic as this trail has been thus far, two of its best spots are yet to come, an emerald green fern glen at Post 29 and a place where the path passes first through two close growing trees, then through the hollow trunk of a single tree. If you have any warts in need of the Huck Finn spunk-water treatment, look for a little basin in the tremendous bay tree to the left of the path, a few feet farther. Breathe deeply by that bay tree for one of the rainy season's best treats.

Suddenly you are past Post 30 and approaching the parking lot. If you used the trail booklet, please replace it for the next walker. Shake the rain from your shoulders and go home feeling refreshed.

In Tilden Park, the Little Farm is great to visit on a rainy day or en route to the Wildcat Trail or Jewel Lake Trail.

28 _Like a knoll of hairy trolls, this cluster of cacti at the University of California Botanical Garden seem to be of another wordly community._

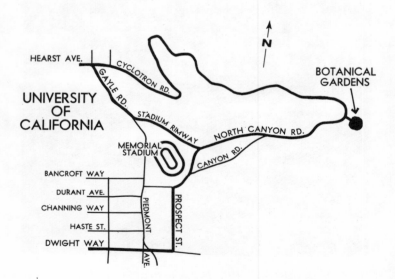

A Canyon Full of Flowers

■ There may not be any warlike triffyds in the University of California Botanical Garden in Berkeley, but it's probably only because they took the wrong turn at the stadium.

Certainly a thousand other kinds of plants seem to be there. There's a whole community of comic fat cacti, long, gauche ones like vegetables designed by Modigliani and knolls of hairy trolls. Wild flowers and tame gossip across the paths. A tree whose leaves seem to be anchors grows on the hillside.

An acacia with built-in tents for fire-ants flourishes in the greenhouse near a vine with traps like pitchers and another with straps like roots. Some of the roots seem to be fruits. Flowers may be leaves and leaves thorns, but whether you know aureoles from petioles, or a puya from a hole in the ground, this is really the California "where bowers of flowers bloom in the sun."

It is open to the public 364 days of the year, all but Christmas, and the walking is choice indeed. Like a trip through the zoo, there is something to see at every turn of the path.

Begin this walk a mile and a half east uphill from the main campus on North Canyon Road just beyond the Strawberry Canyon recreational area. (The tennis courts, playing fields, clubhouse and swimming pools here are open only to University people.) Park by the greenhouses and stop in the office for a guide map of the grounds.

To see coffee, tea, banana and vanilla plants, and the strange acacia from Mexico, visit the tropic glass house.

(Other greenhouses are full of research projects which may be inspected on weekdays by groups making special arrangements in advance. Phone THornwall 5-6000, extension 3343, to set up a guided tour.) The glass houses are all descendants of a frothy one much like the Conservatory in Golden Gate Park which stood in Dr. E. W. Hilgaard's time where Haviland Hall is now.

From the tropic house, follow the nearby path between African Hill and the succulent garden through the old bold shapes of saguaro and organ cactus to reach a pond, with surrounding bushes of rhododendron, azalea and camellias. The waterfall is Strawberry Creek, issuing from the hill for a careen through 25 acres at the canyon head before being piped underground again. Look on your left in the Eurasian area to find that big thorny anchor tree.

At the second fork in the path, bear right downhill past an Australasian area. Visible uphill are the experimental gardens where the late Dr. Harper Goodspeed, long the director of the gardens, and his longtime associate, botanist P. C. Hutchison, a plant hunter in the Andes, did their definitive research on tobacco. On weekdays, a walker may come upon scientists at work in the garden, sometimes with students in attendance. As you walk, notice the benches and picnic tables thoughtfully placed in sheltered locations.

At the herb gardens, a special delight for gastronomes, follow the main path right. Just before you reach the restrooms, there is another path on the right that leads into the lawns where students often sun or study.

To find an area where there are more wildflowers in a single concentration than you are likely to see in a weekend of driving these days, return to the main path and walk uphill toward the succulent gardens again. When you are abreast of the lath house, walk left past small pools into the California area. Near the hill crest, look uphill to try to spot the fire road that circles the canyon, a real workout for gungho hikers.

The gardener toiling near you could be manager Anton Christ or his assistant Al Irving. If you're a botany buff, for this walk forget your field guide and bring a notebook instead. Not only is every plant named, but the tags often give information about primitive uses as well.

The tall saguaro cacti look like Modigliani had a hand in their design. As western movies sometimes show, these grow taller than a horse and rider.

29

In Piedmont's Cherry Walk, trees in bloom make an unforgetable spring-time experience. Piedmont Park was once a health resort.

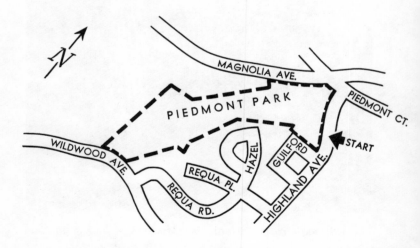

A Cherry Tree Walk

- "And since for seeing trees in bloom/fifty years is little room," wrote A. E. Housman in *A Shropshire Lad*, "about the orchard I will go/to see the cherries hung with snow."

In Piedmont Park in the heart of Piedmont, a town of 1.8 square miles totally surrounded by the less elegant city of Oakland, Housman would be enchanted. Farsighted little Piedmont, instead of destroying its existing amenities to accommodate freeways, has re-established the Cherry Tree Walk.

To see for yourself, come to the corner of Highland Avenue and Guilford Road when it is cherry-blossom time in Piedmont. Cross Highland into Piedmont Park.

There an enticing path meanders through a few old and many new young plantings of Yoshino and Beni Hoshi cherry trees foaming in pink and white "seas of bloom, of soft perfume, of sweet perfume" as another poet, Alfred Noyes, once described the cherry trees of Kew Gardens in London. The Yoshinos make the umbrella-like canopies of flowers. The taller Beni Hoshis reach up their branches jubilantly, like a paean of praise to spring.

As you follow the pathway, look for eight gnarled old Yoshinos, all that is left of a planting of 17 given in 1932 by Mrs. Walter Starr to establish the Cherry Tree Walk for the Piedmont Garden Club in honor of the Bicentennial of George Washington's birthday.

These valiant survivors of a long period of civic indifference inspired the club to save the remaining trees in 1961. Club members approached the Piedmont Park and Street

Department to tidy up the underbrush and prune eight old redwoods and two great pines, survivors of the Piedmont Sulphur Springs spa whose grounds the trees graced.

Once it had been cleaned, the women were so impressed with the potential, they brought in landscape designer Helen Newbauer Selby to plan a renovation based on the existing trees. Then they went to work to raise money to pay for it.

Pause for a moment on one of the benches and look about. (The benches, incidentally, were made with thrift John McLaren or any Scot would admire—from a tree that had fallen.) The tremendous old Tudor-style house bordering the park on the south was the residence of the late Joseph Knowland.

Notice near the end of the looping path a small Community Center building. This is the formal entrance to the park.

A Japanese garden, the earliest of forerunners to the Cherry Tree Walk, once stood in the area of the path, an adjunct to the Piedmont Hotel built here in 1876 after Walter Blair and Samuel Howe extended their Oakland horse car line to the Piedmont hills.

Go behind the center to find old grottoes, benches, waterfalls and a totally unexpected wild canyon whose stream is crossed by several bridges. In the 1850s, when this land was farmed by a Mr. Reed, white sulphur springs similar to those near Napa gushed down here. Among others to have benefitted was a Mr. Holman, one-time congressman from South Carolina, who is reputed to have bathed there to cure his rheumatism. According to *Queen of the Hills*, a Piedmont history by Evelyn Craig Pattiani, later developers discovered in the canyon "the bathtub he had used in his self-treatment" and decided to build a health resort.

The Cherry Tree Walk ends near the Community Center, but the park continues on down the canyon below Piedmont Junior High School, ending near the football field. Loop down one side and back on the other for one more look when the cherry, "the loveliest of trees," is heavy with blossoms.

The Piedmont cherry trees are the highlight of Spring's blooming season.

30

Lake Merritt was once an arm of San Antonio Creek. Now it has become one of Oakland's most appreciated amenities.

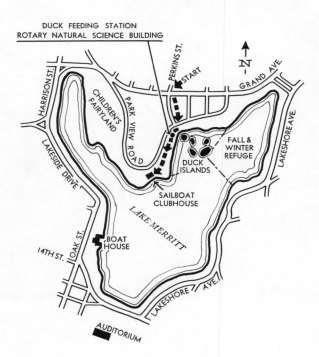

By the Lake in Oakland

■ Oakland's Lake Merritt, a natural salt water lake of about 150 acres made by damming the north arm of San Antonio Creek, as the Oakland Estuary was originally known, has been a state game refuge since 1870. It was the first of its kind on the North American continent.

From the time in 1915 when the first flock of ducks got a meal here, they and their fine feathered friends have been constant in their appreciation. Annually more than 4000 migratory birds of some 75 species on the Pacific Flyway check in here for a visit.

Among them are the buffleheads, greenheads and bald-pates, the helldivers, greater and lesser scaups, double-crested cormorants, marbled godwits, coots, loons, spoonbills, ruddy ducks and the common tern.

Despite all this waterfowl activity, Lakeside Park offers one of the most urbane strolls in the Bay Area.

Begin this walk at the corner of Grand Avenue and Perkins Street. Follow Perkins southeasterly into the park where a long curving block meets Bellevue near the water's edge. Ducky noises from the haunts of the coot and tern will be audible as you approach the Rotary Natural Science Building.

Enter it to see a hive of bees under glass in one wall, a candy-colored, streamlined, spotted gila monster, a mean weasel, a silky mole, turtles, iguanas and other small beasts.

Once outside again, stroll toward the brooder cage, which looks like a great white plastic chunk of watermelon in which downy ducklings are protected until they outgrow the hors d'oeuvre size most tempting to seagulls. A rare resident golden eagle, great horned owl and other unusual predators live in the hexagonal cages 10 steps away.

Walk over to the shoreline and look for the trumpeter swan on one or another of the five man-made islands which look like outsize Easter nests offshore. Then glance west to see the Kiwanis Kiddy Korner keeping up with the Rotarians with unusual seahorse swings for toddlers.

Older people will want to meander instead in an easterly pattern around the largest bird corral in the general direction of the flight cage, a geodesic dome designed by Buckminster Fuller and erected in one day. It is 30 feet across and the wide mesh of the screening permits small birds to fly through.

Larger birds nest in those standing globes. The favorite with park regulars here is a talking magpie named Lady, who sometimes asks "Where are the children?" Coyotes, wolves, foxes, porcupines and such are in the modular junior zoo cages nearby.

The "Duck Dinner 10 Cents" in the dispensers is grain. Hungry walkers will find better fare for humans inside the Lakeside Inn, whose tables overlook the bird refuge.

In times past, Lake Merritt, once called Lake Peralta but renamed for a Mayor, Dr. Samuel Merritt, who dammed San Antonio Creek, was not always so scenic. Early Oaklanders called it a "cesspool," and claimed "even a sea turtle couldn't swim in it!" When a later, equally visionary mayor, Melvin C. Chapman, acquired the lake, he was accused of wasting taxpayers' money.

Today it is the amenity most prized by Oaklanders.

When you've had a surfeit of ducks, go behind Lakeside Inn to find three other good activities. A trackless train that rolls its eyes and gives out with wolf-whistles runs between here and Children's Fairyland, a good walk in itself anytime. No adults are admitted unless accompanied by a child.

At the sailboat clubhouse about a block from the Inn, where all the little El Toros put in, there are two excursion boats, the *Cabrillo* and the *Portola,* leaving on the hour and on the half. One can tour the lake for the modest sum of 25 cents.

If flowers are your pleasure, cross Bellevue instead, to enjoy the gardens which surround the Garden Center. The blase can always find a bench or a bit of grass on which to watch as others enjoy the rites of spring.

This spherical cage houses a wide variety of birds at the Lake Merritt Sanctuary.

Bret Harte Boardwalk is close to Oakland's Jack London Square. The author of "The Luck of Roaring Camp" used to pass here on his way to school.

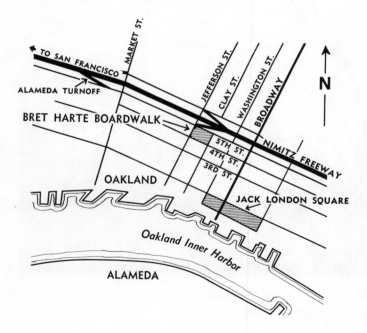

Where Bret Harte Used to Walk

■ A hundred years ago a man from Oakland bestowed romance on the scruffy, unshorn, red-shirted, flea-bitten, gold-seeking miners of 1849 and gave California its first taste of international literary prestige, all in one beau geste.

His name was Bret Harte. He did it with a story called *The Luck of Roaring Camp* that appeared in the August 1868 issue of *The Overland Monthly*.

Coincidentally it was also Bret Harte who drew the railroad tracks under the totem grizzly on *The Overland Monthly's* title page, converting with two lines a lonely, pointless bear into a symbol that is meaningful even today.

His adopted home town of Oakland, which he dearly loved, appeared in many of Bret Harte's stories as Encinal, an early Spanish name for the same land.

Typical of towns, Oakland gave this talented resident short shrift until 1962. Then Mrs. Paul Mills and Mrs. Herbert M. Stoll, both associated with the Oakland Art Museum, resurrected a little clutch of old houses they have called Bret Harte Boardwalk.

Bret Harte may have walked by them many a time, thwanging a stick against fence pickets as boys will, for the house in which he lived with his mother and stepfather, Colonel Andrew Williams, at one time Mayor of Oakland, stood just across the street on the northwest corner of Fifth and Clay.

There is a pleasant stroll awaiting historians, shoppers, diners and just plain walkers on the Bret Harte Boardwalk.

To reach the Boardwalk from San Francisco, take the

Alameda turnoff from the Nimitz Freeway, Highway 17, onto Fifth Street. Follow Fifth straight ahead to Jefferson. You will then be at Bret Harte Boardwalk, which faces Fifth (and the freeway underpinnings which have replaced Harte's home) between Jefferson and Clay Streets.

Park behind the Boardwalk on Fourth or Third Street and walk around to the joyful gold and white buildings. Go up the low stairs to the wooden walk that has unified the once-dilapidated old homes into an exciting mercantile compound.

"The homes were built within five blocks of the estuary upon whose bank the city of Oakland was first planted," according to a report by historian Augustin C. Keane in the magazine for the National Trust for Historic Preservation.

"Since 1850 the city has grown and moved away from the antiquated dwellings. They, together with a scattering of shabby, low-income residences, were left behind amidst sheds and warehouses and industrial buildings." When Mrs. Mills and Mrs. Stoll happened upon them, the houses "stood bleak and forlorn, begrimed, with shattered windows and debris piling up about them."

As you browse, notice the vitality of both shops and names. Roaring Camp Mercantile, the Hitching Post and Colonel Starbottle are all derivative from the Bret Harte stories. To see a portrait of Andrew Williams, the stepfather from whom Bret Harte drew Colonel Culpepper Starbottle, go into the bar. Look also on other walls for artifacts and ephemera that would do a museum proud. The brick warehouse-like building was built by W. Armand Boyerval, once cellarmaster to Count Haraszthy, pioneer California wine grower.

After you have explored upstairs and down, from the antiques and gimcracks to the nonsense and saucy books, pause in the outdoor patio for lunch and then if you are still eager for more walking, walk two blocks south and four west to reach another, larger plaza, Jack London Square.

The waterfront is at the foot of Broadway. Boats chug by. Trains pass and the walking is pleasantly exciting.

32 *Jack London Square has fakery too, but it's all goodnatured and keeps the human dimension.*

Oakland's Wonderful Waterfront

■ Jack London Square, Oakland's glamorous industrial waterfront, has so much "there" there, it can quite confidently make Fisherman's Wharf look to its laurels.

Where on Fisherman's Wharf, for example, can one dip fingers or toes in the water? Step on tidal rock in its natural water-washed place? Sit outdoors in comfort without having hawkers push their touristy wares?

By contrast, at Jack London Square, man's natural affinity for enjoying the water's edge has been built right into the grander plan.

To see for yourself, come for a walk on Oakland's waterfront. AC Transit line 11 is the dependable bus to get you there from downtown Oakland. Disembark at the foot of Broadway and look around to get your bearings. Notice the large trees, the separation of traffic from pedestrians, the absence of barkers and shouting signs.

This spot is where metropolitan Oakland began, as Hildegarde Hawthorne wrote in *Romantic Cities of California,* "in chicanery, ruthless expropriation, disregard of other people's rights." The bad hats were a triumvirate of landgrabbers, Edson Adams, Andrew Moon and Horace Carpentier. It was Carpentier who built the first dock on this site in 1851. He also arranged to be Oakland's first Mayor and to hold a franchise for the ferry service to San Francisco at $1 per trip.

Walk west past the firehouse, the photogenic old anchor, and the electrified gas light to see the fireboat *City of Oakland,* where she lies at anchor. Notice the benches by the firehouse and the wooden walk by the pleasant boatel.

As you walk, look across the estuary to see a Coast Guard cutter, berthed here—unless she is off on an errand of mercy. Near at hand are small boats, such as the *Whosoever* and the *Shin Pai Nai*.

When you reach 5 Jack London Square, an old warehouse or godown now remodeled into offices for attorneys and architects, go out on its pierlike veranda to see one or another ship being scrubbed. Notice the yellow ark, the two-masted schooner, the homes of artists. Here, secretaries often lunch on the rocks while dangling their toes in the water.

Retrace your steps back to the Bow and Bell, but skirt it and go on along the water's edge toward the Sea Wolf restaurant and the reconstructed ferryboat, faked up to look like a Mississippi steamer. Continue east and you'll find that the wooden walk ends here. For a long time the Fish Grotto was the only one at Jack London Square. Now there is a wide choice.

Notice the outside elevator on another old remodeled warehouse. Walk out on the marina along a benchlined pier toward the Spice Box to find a shop where boatmen pick up sandwiches. Then head back, bearing ever easterly, to find Johnson and Joseph, ship chandlers, publishers of the little historical newspaper, *The Clipper*, and beyond it Heinhold's First and Last Chance Saloon, where Jack London's memory is preserved in cobwebs and smoke-blackened mementoes carefully protected under chickenwire, a touch that would have pleased the old socialist.

There are also shops, a gaudy Japanese garden, railroad tracks on which passing trains rumble by and other goodies. Linger awhile and seek them out, for this is not a place where one feels pushed or pressured. As the ships come and go, almost in reaching distance, the thoughtful walker may discover again that human dimension that can make a city pleasurable.

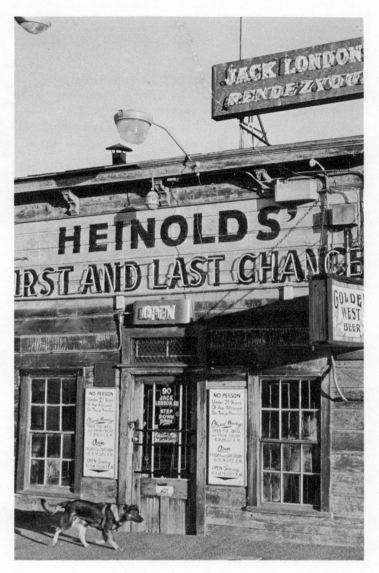

This was Jack London's favorite pub. Everything else in the area has been gussied up so much London would never recognize it today.

33 *Pt. Richmond from Nicholl Nob overlooks the Richmond Bridge and Standard Oil's long wharf. Keller's Beach is nearest point of land immediately below hill.*

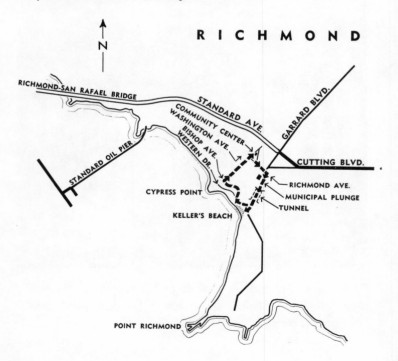

A Little Slice of Yesterday

■ The community of Point Richmond sits on the Contra Costa like a little piece of yesterday that floated across the bay and stranded itself when the tide went out.

An urbane, attractive oasis in a vast and otherwise depressing industrial steppe, it perches on hills that climb up from the water, like Sausalito, gently tree-shaded and eminently liveable. At its heart is a focal triangle of unusual shops and restaurants. On its shore is a new public park, one of the rare waterside parks on the bay. The walk of exploration could make a pleasant Sunday.

Begin this walk by transporting yourself to the vicinity via State Route 17 as if you were going to cross the Richmond-San Rafael Bridge.

The Point Richmond turnoff is left from Cutting Boulevard at Garrard, and you don't get much of a crack at it in traffic. As landmarks, keep an eye peeled for the Point Orient restaurant, the big Richmond Municipal Plunge, or for the tunnels by it. Not much more than 60 years ago 1200 acres of this sprawling industrial slurb was blue bay water surrounding Ellis Landing.

Point Richmond itself was an island until Jacob Tewksbury dammed it to start the shoaling and fill. A. S. MacDonald gets the credit or blame for enticing Santa Fe railroad to make Richmond its Bay Area terminal. Pullman cars were also built nearby in the heyday of passenger trains.

At the outset, park near the triangle defined by Washington Avenue, Park Street and Richmond Avenue. In the core of the triangle are two municipal buildings, one housing the fire department, the other a community center and library.

Then browse the periphery, a colorful conglomeration that includes the Santa Fe Market, a name that bespeaks the origin of the town, Masquer's Playhouse, Icthus Coffee House and Gallery, named for the secret sign used for the 300 years when Christianity was an underground movement, the Famous Original Hotel Mac, known for its good food and racy past, a remodeled old firehouse, containing five tasteful shops, one modestly called The Shop Upstairs, another flamboyantly titled Pablo Fanque's Fair.

Look for Luther Malone, who makes and repairs violins, the stained glass windows of the Baltic Bar which keep their promise with rich mahogany and classical saloon nudes within.

The Cantonese Point Orient, the Mexican Inn and Jumbo's Burgers all have more than countywide following. Look uphill to spot four nearby churches.

Then for unexpected contrast to this sophisticated little outpost, walk on Richmond Avenue to Garrard, the point at which the municipal tunnel goes under Nicholl Nob, just past the plunge. Observe as you enter the tunnel the faded letters that say this is the way to the San Francisco ferry. Walk through to emerge at Keller's Beach, a park complete with picnic tables, cliffside trees, a sandy sun trap and a rare chance to dip a toe into bay water. Tarry a while in the sun.

Off to the north is Standard Oil's Long Wharf. The mechanized buzz in the southern distance is the Richmond Ramblers Motorcycle Club, which has a hill to climb a mile away. Jutting into the water is Ferry Point, used by Santa Fe tugs and barges for shuttling box cars to the City.

Automobile and passenger ferry service could be reinstated with a minimum of trauma here.

As the shadows lengthen, follow Western Avenue to Bishop, then start uphill on Washington which will take you up over the ridge to return you to the shopping area. Moun-

tain goats who would look both ways from the saddle of hills
can digress a few blocks south on Crest for the view from
Nicholl Nob, now a regional park.

To cap your walk with understanding of this progressive
community, search out a newstand offering the lively-minded
little weekly newspaper, *Point Counterpoint, a Journal for
Civic Communication,* whose motto could well be "All good
taste costs is courage."

*Point Richmond has a flavor all its own and its downtown
triangle of old buildings housing interesting shops enhances
it. This former firehouse shelters a genuine soda fountain,
several boutiques and antique marts. One shop at the back
is in a remodeled jail.*

34

Hikers along the main California Riding and Hiking Trail festoon the great long western slope of Mount Diablo. Once all the hills of the Bay Area were bare.

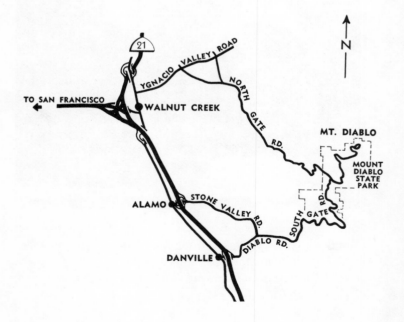

Take a Walk With a View

■ Almost every winter, there is a gloriously clear morning on which the Bay Area awakens to discover new snow glistening whitely on the double peaks of Mount Diablo, the jewel of Contra Costa County. Then for San Franciscans who seldom see snow, and especially for nostalgic expatriate midwesterners, it is time for a walk around the south peak of Diablo.

At 3841 feet above sea level, Diablo, along with Mount Tamalpais in Marin, dominates the Bay Area. In 1862 William H. Brewer, a member of the official California survey field party, estimated that from Diablo's summit it was possible to see "spread out in tolerably plain view—over 300 miles from north to south and 260 miles from east to west."

With today's ever-increasing smog, it is unlikely that the walker will see that far, yet given a clear day, the trip is worth the effort. For lack of a well-planned summit-loop observation trail, begin this walk by driving to the parking lot at the summit west of the lookout building.

Mount Diablo State Park seems discouragingly dedicated to the automobile and other mechanical devices, rather than to people, especially those on foot, so reconcile yourself to walking on the road. Follow the road uphill at an easy grade to the stone observation building.

The building itself is worth a little inspection since it was built from fossiliferous upper Miocene sandstone quarried near the south gate in 1931, shortly after Diablo became a state park. Space inside once devoted to a museum has been usurped by a ranger's living quarters.

The devil which gave Diablo its name is neither of the ugly communications monsters near the crest, but an Indian evil spirit or "puy," reputed to have helped the Bolgones Indians defeat a military expedition from the Spanish presidio in San Francisco in 1806.

North Peak, privately owned, obscures the view north. Look south and west to see San Ramon and Diablo Valleys, and southeast to see Livermore Valley. Peaks you can see include the Sierra, the Cascades, Mount St. Helena and Mount Hamilton.

In 1851, Diablo was chosen as the base point for U.S. surveys of California and a meridian line through the peak near the tower establishes other locations. "The great features of the view lie to the east of the meridian passing through the peak," wrote Brewer.

"First, the great central valley of California, as level as the sea, stretches to the horizon both on the north and to the southeast . . . on the north are the Marysville Buttes, rising like black masses from the plain, over a hundred miles distant; while still beyond, rising in sharp clear outline against the sky, stand the snow-covered Lassen's Buttes (Mount Lassen) over 200 miles in air line distant from us. . . .

"Rising from this great plain, and forming the horizon for 300 miles in extent, possibly more, were the snowy crests of the Sierra Nevada. What a grand sight! The peaks of that mighty chain glittering in the purest white under the bright sun, their icy crests seeming a fitting helmet for their black and furrowed sides!"

Closer at hand, the odd formation east of the tower is known as the Devil's Pulpit. According to the State Division of Mines *Geologic Guidebook of the Bay Area*, "Mount Diablo is a sort of geologic freak. The core of the twin-peaked mountain consists of jumbled massive rocks of the Franciscan formation which literally have been punched through the once-overlying Cretaceous and Miocene formations from below. Upturned edges of these ruptured formations flank the mountain on every side and a large fault zone can be followed around the base." Geologists interpret this to mean that Diablo, high as it is now, was once a sea bottom.

If you yearn to come back to explore the mountain more intimately, pick up the Clayton and Diablo quadrangle maps, 7½-minute series of the Federal Geological Survey. The hiking trails on park maps issued at the gate are inaccurate and except near the roads trails are unmarked.

Bring your own first aid kit. Rattlers are not uncommon on Diablo, and in at least one recent episode there wasn't a snake bite kit available in the park. For some odd reason, park headquarters is closed on weekends, the time of heaviest use.

From the fire lookout tower on the crest of Mount Diablo, one can survey the entire Bay Area, smog permitting. Snow decorates this 3841' peak sometime during almost every winter.

145

35

*Hidden Valley contains vineyards in the lee of Mission Peak.
Olive trees border the pinot chardonnay vines on the road
from Mission San Jose.*

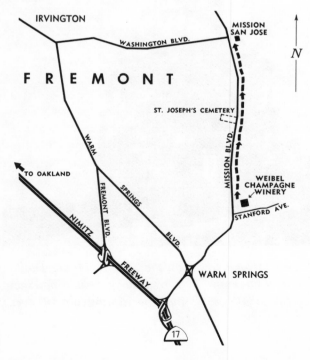

Hidden in the Valley

■ Spring is a caress that wakens this bright land into eloquent, simple beauty. As fair as any is the valley that shelters Mission San Jose at the base of the 2508-foot Mission Peak near the southeasternmost finger of San Francisco Bay. Here one can still walk near orchards in bloom and vineyards in new leaf, smell their lush perfumes, hear the clear-throated meadowlark and the hum of bees and, best of all, enjoy the seasonal reassurance of life-resurgent.

In this time when freeways and housing tracts gobble acres of irreplaceable farmland, Hidden Valley has more for the visitor to see than most. For the walker who is game for an easy two-mile hike, this outing can include winetasting and touring, picnicking and spa inspection, seasoned with a dollop of history and religion.

For those who come by public transportation, overshoot Mission San Jose by two miles on Highway 9-21 en route to Warm Springs and ask the bus driver to let you off at Weibel Champagne Winery, Hidden Valley Ranch or the Stanford Winery Historical Marker, whichever landmark he recognizes. They are all within ten yards of the same tree-lined country lane, Stanford Avenue, which was once the entrance to Rancho del Agua Caliente, granted in 1836 to Fulgencio Higuera.

Walk toward Mission Peak along this country lane between the silvery olive trees and the tender green of pinot chardonnay vines. The trees may have been planted by the Ohlone Indians, but the vines were planted by Rudolph and Fred Weibel, natives of Switzerland, who began their American winemaking career in 1936 in the basement of the William Tell Hotel on Clay Street, San Francisco.

Soon the walker comes upon an historical marker beside a chalet-like cottage. The marker describes earlier ownership of the land by Senator Leland Stanford. The cottage is the Weibel Hacienda, a tasting room to which the public is welcome. A long-time winemaker, Bert Salazar, presides here and conducts tours.

If you can tear yourself away from this well-gardened spot, continue to the end of the lane to the hodgepodge of buildings and picnic tables now called Hidden Valley Ranch, also open to the public, but much in need of an inspired redevelopment genius.

In 1850, Clement Columbet created a fashionable resort around five of the hot springs which gave Agua Caliente its name, and the name of Warm Springs to a nearby South Bay landing. San Franciscans who wished "to take the waters" would travel in Captain Calvin Valpey's steamer most of the way, then finish the trip by stage or on foot.

When Columbet, and later Stanford, operated the spa, the water temperature was 98 degrees, and the springs produced each day about 50,000 gallons of water rich in soda, borax and sulphur. Its underground source of heat was one of the casualties of the 1906 earthquake.

To visit Mission San Jose, founded in 1797 and the site of one of the few remaining Spanish or Mexican adobes in the Bay Area, retrace your steps to the end of the lane and bear north on the west side of the main road, Highway 9-21. En route you may observe a trap or skeet shoot in progress at one point, or pause to rest in St. Joseph's Cemetery, whose headstones reveal that many of the pioneers in this area were Portuguese.

If it amuses you, you may also listen for cornet music. One of Mission San Jose's pioneer tales revolves around two friends, a Mr. Lockwood and a Mr. Beard, both of Indiana. On setting out for California, Lockwood gave his friend a cornet, saying: "I understand California is a very wooded country and we may have trouble finding each other; but take this horn with you and blow it occasionally. In this way we can locate each other." As kooky as it sounds, Lockwood ultimately located his friend by tooting his own cornet on the Mission embarcadero.

Old Mission San Jose uses its adobe, once the priest's house, as a museum, and it is well worth the modest 25-cent fee just to look at the splendid embroidered cape once worn by Fray Junipero Serra. Since the Greyhound bus depot is just across the street, it is possible to while away waiting time exploring the Mission and its grounds.

At Mission San Jose this adobe, once a priests' house, is now a museum. Inside are relics of early Spanish and Mexican habitation and records of pioneer settlement in Washington Township.

149

36

Coyote Hills Regional Park is close to the San Mateo Bridge, has trails to wander, Indian Mounds to explore and a Bio-Sonar Laboratory to visit.

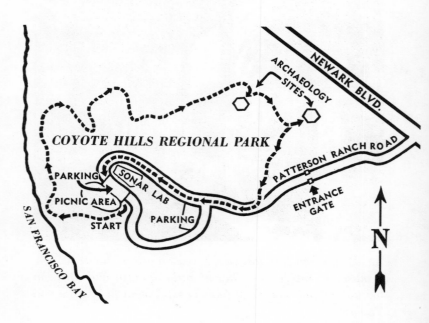

Hills by the Salt Marshes

■ "All day," Fray Pedro Font wrote in his diary in April, 1776, "the commander and I have been in doubt as to whether the island at the end of the estuary which I mapped yesterday is really an island or not."

The supposed island that puzzled Captain Juan Bautista de Anza's party was Coyote Hills on the eastern shore of San Francisco Bay. Many a motorist driving across the Dumbarton Bridge must also have puzzled on this one elevated area in miles of flat terrain, wondered "what do you suppose is up there?" and resolved to go someday and find out.

What is up there today is 1000 acres of public playground, the Coyote Hills Regional Park. There are shallow bays where fish spawn. Intertidal mudflats where live the small invertebrates on which shore birds, terns, ducks and gulls feed. There are salt marshes and natural bay shores which include the plants essential to many birds and small mammals. There are families of harbor seals. There are Indian mounds under excavation by several colleges.

There is the Stanford Research Institute Bio-Sonar Laboratory taking signals from seals and sea lions. There is an abandoned missile site. Trails meander along the shoreline above salt flats and ramble up the hillcrest, overlooking a rare portion of San Francisco Bay. Father Font could still recognize it if he came this way again.

There is also a six-mile trail for hikers, bikers and horsemen from Coyote Hills to the mouth of Niles Canyon, a unit in the projected 500-mile chain of trails through the hills that form the eastern flank of the bay.

To make an exploratory excursion, head south on the Bayshore from San Francisco. The park lies on the Alameda County shoreline between the San Mateo Bridge and the Dumbarton Bridge. Access is via Patterson Ranch Road, a paved lane which turns west from Union City-Newark Boulevard between Jarvis Avenue in Newark and West Jackson Street in Mount Eden. Nimitz Freeway (Highway 17) is the easy way to arrive from the East Bay.

From the entrance gate, follow the road uphill around a curve overlooking the Bio-Sonar Lab to a parking lot adjacent to a picnic area snuggled in trees against the eastern slope of the center hill. Elevation about 200 feet. As you pass the lab, check at its gates to find the visiting hours.

Then park and walk south along the upper road to find a trail on your right that goes west over the crest of the hill for a sensational view of the bay. The J. P. Munro-Fraser *History of Alameda County* credits John Quigley and F. A. Plummer as the early pioneers in salt making at Union City.

The *Second Report of the State Mineralogist of California, 1880* indicates that the early settlers were gathering salt from natural reservoirs filled at high tide and sun-dried later as early as 1848. Indians may have taught them, for the Indian kitchen middens on these shores, according to an estimate by Dr. Adan Treganza, may go back 4000 years.

To see one of the excavated mounds, follow the trail north, then up over the hill and down across the flat near the flood control channel. Two of the sites, in which archeologists have been working for 20 years, thanks to the scientific interest and good will of the Patterson family, whose land this was, are open on weekends for the public to inspect. (Use the clumps of trees in the flat lands for your landmark as you walk.)

When you have marvelled at the odd burial postures of exposed bones, walk south to pick up the road and make a loop back to the picnic area. The round trip is about three miles. Walking boots and jeans and a Thermos are recommended.

*Coyote Hills Regional Park in Alameda County has a trail
for hikers, bikers and horsemen. It goes six miles from the
mouth of Niles Canyon to the Bay.*

Peninsula

37

Thorton Beach plunges down from high cliffs just south from San Francisco. It is also a point where the San Andreas fault reaches the sea.

A Beach With a Giant Fault

■ The great heaving land that is California seems to have a few jokes of its own. One of these, a repeated setting for history's own comic operas, is Thornton Beach.

The northernmost of the 11 choice sand pockets that are included in San Mateo Beaches State Park, Thornton Beach is just west of the junction where Alemany Boulevard ends at Skyline Boulevard. Its first joke on mere man is that this is where the San Andreas fault pushes into the sea.

To explore Thornton Beach, start early in the morning, for the parking lot on a fair day is apt to fill up by 1 p.m. Bring the day-use fee (50¢ per car during the winter season, 25¢ anytime for walkers) and a picnic. Then drive down what was part of old State Highway 1 until the 1957 land-slide, making the hairpin turn that takes one to the beach proper. Park your car, walk down the ramp, then go south on the beach toward Mussel Rock.

According to geologists Clyde Wahrhaftig, J. Schlocker and M. G. Bonilla, who prepared a series of ten geological walks for the California Division of Mines and Geology (available at the Ferry Building for 50¢), the things to be seen here include: "(1) the point where the San Andreas fault reaches the sea; (2) landslides, quite active in 1906, where the fault reaches the sea; (3) tract houses draped around the headwalls of these landslides and in places on them; (4) numerous examples of landslides and beach ero-sion where the Coast Highway had to be abandoned."

Dedicated amateurs of geology will especially want to consult this leaflet for a description by N. Timothy Hall of the baleen whale bones and pelecypod and gastropod fossils exposed in Thornton Beach cliffs.

Historians may be more interested, as they walk this beach, in the opera bouffe of R. S. Thornton, the young farmer whose property this once was. In 1853, before the Homestead Law, the stretch of rolling hills between Rancho Laguna de la Merced on the north and Rancho Buri Buri on the south was sold in small parcels by the U. S. Government. Most of the buyers were young veterans of the Mexican War, who used their war service bonus land bounty certificates to buy 40 to 60 acres.

Imagine the howls the morning they discovered surveyors from the big rancho to the north, greedy for these little vegetable farms. As professor Frank Stanger tells it in *South from San Francisco*, "They fortified a barn with bags of potatoes, set up a brass cannon and prepared to defy the sheriff's posse. There was almost a 'Battle of Colma' to go down in history. But the besieged were persuaded to abandon this tactic, and their redoubt as well. Instead they organized the North San Mateo Settlers' Union and elected one of their number, R. S. Thornton, to conduct the necessary legal battle."

After years in Washington, seeing the fight through the Supreme Court, Thornton returned victorious, and in May of 1866 the settlers were allowed to reoccupy their farms.

From the beach, railroad buffs can look uphill and see in the imagination the little excursion cars of the ill-fated Ocean Shore Railroad, puffing along against the cliff. Highway 1 was first laid out on its roadbed. In 1905 the railroad built sections south from San Francisco and north from Santa Cruz.

"It reaches the beaches," its advertising proclaimed, but it never reached them all and the two halves of the railroad never met. The big barriers were Devil's Slide and San Pedro Point. To surmount them, The Ocean Shore ferried excursionists between Tunitas and Swanton (now Davenport Landing) via a Stanley Steamer automobile.

Of course, it doesn't have to be amusing if you're not in the mood to be amused. "There is a rapture on the lonely shore/ There is society where none intrudes/ By the deep sea, and music in its roar," wrote George Noel Gordon, Lord Byron, phrasing the sea hunger for thousands of less-articulate people who yearn for the shore.

Thornton Beach has this music, too.

Thornton Beach is the northernmost of all 11 San Mateo County Beaches, each with its own pleasures for sand walkers, surfers, fishermen and picnickers.

38

Portola and his men rode horseback from Point San Pedro up this ridge for their first look at San Francisco Bay. They were disappointed, it wasn't Monterey.

The Walk of Discovery

■ Romantics make much of the first ships to sail into San Francisco Bay, as well they might, for these journeys were great feats of derring-do. But the persistent truth is that the bay was first spotted by Europeans on foot. From land. While searching for something else.

Specifically by deer hunters November 2, 1769 from an overlook we now call Sweeney Ridge in San Mateo County.

They were part of the overland expedition led by Don Gaspar de Portola to find Monterey, who had camped that day at Point San Pedro. It didn't create much of a stir in camp when the hunters returned with their report. Ho hum. It wasn't Monterey.

Nevertheless, the chaplain and diarist, Fray Juan Crespi, dutifully recorded that they had seen to northward "an immense arm of the sea or an estuary which penetrated into the land as far as the eye could reach, extending to the southeast; that they had seen some beautiful plains well adorned with trees, and that the smoke which they saw in all directions left no doubt that the country was thickly populated with heathen villages." Two days later, after the return of a scouting party, the entire expedition made its way up Sweeney Ridge.

For walkers two centuries later there is an exceptional opportunity to climb Sweeney Ridge through beautiful rangeland usually closed to the public. The vistas are just as spectacular for the rediscoverers as they were in Portola's time.

To make this walk transport yourself via Highway 1 to

the Rockaway Beach neighborhood of Pacifica. Go uphill on Sea Bowl Drive to Fassler Avenue. When you reach Crespi Elementary School, park, put on your walking shoes, pocket your lunch and walk uphill to 1166 Fassler Avenue where the pavement ends.

Locate the red sign which says "Private Property. Discovery site. Hikers must obtain permit from Pacifica Beaches and Recreation Department, City Hall." A blanket permit for walkers has been issued through the good offices of Grace McCarthy, since Pacifica is negotiating for this property for a park. So take happily to the open road.

The first part is the steep part of this climb. As you walk, notice the straw that has been strewn over the water line from the nearby tank. This is to forestall erosion. At the tank, take the right fork and continue climbing. About 100 yards beyond, pause for a look south at the Montara mountains to see the saddle the Portola party came through. Another 100 yards will reveal the offshore rocks on Point San Pedro, and the smaller, columnar rocks of Rockaway Beach.

At the second water tank, bear right again. If the going seems steep at this point, take heart. The trail soon levels out to a gradual lift. From starting point to the discovery site, it is 1.8 miles. In June 1969, 500 parents and children, one of them in a baby carriage, made the discovery climb. There have also been moonrise hikes and an Easter Sunrise service held at the discovery site, and local Boy Scouts have climbed from the seashore to the crest as a reenactment of the Portola expedition.

As you walk, try to envision a party of 60 men, some ill with scurvy and slung on improvised stretchers, others on horseback, some herding pack mules. According to historian Frank Stanger, the procession was led by the scout, Sergeant Jose Ortega, followed by the commander, Captain Portola, then other officers and two Franciscan friars. A squad of Catalonian soldiers, some Indians from Lower California, the engineer corps and the packtrain were next on the trail. A

160

rear guard, commanded by Captain Fernando Rivera, completed the procession.

After you pass a missile site box surrounded by a table-like fence, the steep part of the climb is over and one can see San Francisco and Mount Tamalpais to the north. The green patch near the ocean is Sharp Park Golf Course. The white building on a distant peak is the U.S. Coast Guard Station on Sweeney Ridge.

Look again for a red sign when you reach the fence. Go through it and hew to the trail. Hereafter, in each case take the low road. When the trail hits a larger road, cross into the meadow by the red stake. Follow the path uphill.

At the old bed springs, or what remains of them, bear left uphill. Then follow the red stakes, each about 20 feet apart, until you reach the knoll on which there are tremendous letters saying "Portola was here 1769." This whimsy was the contribution of the late Jack O'Marie, a much-loved superintendent of the San Francisco Water District lands. The scattered rocks nearby once made a big X, subsequently changed to "Hi!"

The eucalyptus below, a later Australian contribution to the skyline, did not obscure the Portola party's fine view, as they reached this knoll. They also saw Mount Diablo, sans smog. San Andreas Lake below was a valley 200 years ago. So was Crystal Springs Lake at the time Portola camped in it. Another change that may happen here is a scenic recreational road which has been proposed for Sweeney Ridge.

And who was Sweeney? San Mateo County historians don't seem to know for sure.

39 *Sanchez Adobe was headquarters for the 8,928 acre Rancho San Pedro. Cattle from Mission San Dolores ranged this far.*

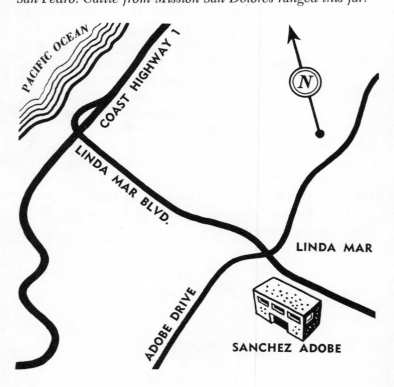

Adobe Among Tract Houses

■ "At every step we came to paths well-beaten by heathen," wrote Fray Francisco Palou in his journal of the expedition conducted in 1774 by Captain Fernando Rivera, an officer of Captain Gaspar de Portola's intrepid band.

"Boylike, he longed to follow one of them," historian Frank Stanger, author of *South from San Francisco*, says, "to see what there is on the shore." Rivera didn't let him, alas.

If he had, there might be a good description existing of the Indian village that once stood uphill from Portola's two-day camp on Pedro Point, at what is now the junction of Linda Mar Boulevard and Adobe Drive in the growing megalopolis called Pacifica.

Historians, and newcomers to the Bay Area who may wonder that so few of the early Indian-Spanish-Mexican vestiges remain on the land, will find a walk around this area rewarding, anyway. Here, half forgotten, is the well-preserved Sanchez Adobe, once the home of Francisco Sanchez, seat of the 8928-acre Rancho San Pedro, and coincidentally, a fine example of authentic Monterey architecture.

To make this walk, transport yourself 11 miles south of San Francisco to the Pedro Valley section of Pacifica via Highway 1. Take the Linda Mar turnoff uphill to Adobe Drive (or walk it if you took the Greyhound). The Sanchez Adobe, which has been used for a hunting lodge, a bootleg saloon and a shed for packing artichokes at low points during the 122 years it has stood here, is now a free museum operated by the San Mateo County Parks and Recreation Commission.

Except on Mondays and Tuesdays, it is open to the public from 10 a.m. to 4 p.m. with an hour's closing at noon so the ranger can have his lunch. If you arrive by miscalculation at 12, the grounds will still be open. Sit down against a wall, pull your hat over your eyes, and take a short siesta. The adobe backdrop is exactly right for that scene.

As you stroll about the five-acre park on which the building is located, try to envision the dancing, music, horsemanship displays and color that existed here when prominent visitors came to see Francisco Sanchez, one-time *commandante* of the Presidio and a former *alcalde* of San Francisco. If 15 miles from the Presidio seems a long way for a man to issue commands, consider that the first European building to stand on this site was a rancho outpost of Mission Dolores, whose cattle ranged this far.

In 1837 the adobe replaced an earlier house built in 1817 with materials salvaged from a ship wrecked on Point San Pedro. In its heydey as a Mission farm, there were 36 acres of wheat, eight acres of corn, an orchard and a vineyard, planted just west of the adobe on what is now the Whites Field playground.

Traces of the earlier Costanoan Indian village disappeared around 1794 when a missionary-introduced epidemic annihilated the native inhabitants.

For the high point of your walk, go inside the building to examine the musem artifacts found nearby, to enjoy the cool of the thick adobe walls if the day is warm, and to stroll the wide upstairs veranda.

Governor Juan B. Alvarado, William Sharon, John C. Fremont, Henry Meiggs, W. C. Ralston, and Hall McAllister are only a few of the history-makers of early California who have surveyed the world from this vantage. (They didn't see the park department workshop building you'll see at the end of the parking lot, however. The routed-wooden signs that are made here supply all Pacifica parks.)

Picnicking is permitted on the lawn by the house, following an old tradition here. The last big *merienda*, or Mexican-style picnic, to be held on the grounds was given by the San Mateo County Historical Society in 1969, the bicentennial of the Portola Expedition. County supervisors bought the historical building and began its restoration in 1947.

The Sanchez Adobe looks toward the saddle through which Portola's men rode on their exploration of the peninsula. Building is classical Monterey architecture and very well preserved. Inside is a museum.

40

Villa Montalvo was Senator Phelan's Home and until 1930, site of an annual "Day in the Hills" where poets read their works and were rewarded with prizes. Now it's a park.

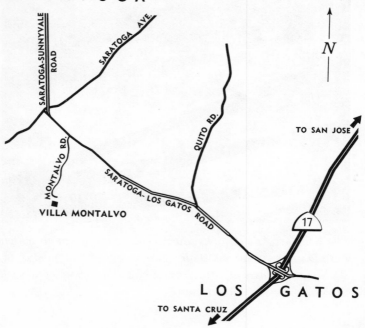

SARATOGA

SARATOGA-SUNNYVALE ROAD

SARATOGA AVE.

QUITO RD.

N

TO SAN JOSE

MONTALVO RD.

SARATOGA-LOS GATOS ROAD

■ **VILLA MONTALVO**

17

LOS GATOS

TO SANTA CRUZ

Italy's Child: Villa Montalvo

■ Tucked away in the foothills of Santa Clara Valley, a half mile south of Saratoga, is a romantic fragment of San Francisco's cultural history called Villa Montalvo. It is a place to stroll a dream. Given half an imaginative chance, garlanded nymphs might dance upon its greensward, or a toga-clad Orpheus wander by, thrumming a lyre, oblivious to time.

"Italy is your mother," Kathleen Norris wrote of Montalvo in 1926, and called it, "this white dream made manifest." Robinson Jeffers, Edwin Markham, Joaquin Miller, Elsie Janis, George Sterling, Ina Coolbrith, Charles Caldwell Dobie, Charles Warren Stoddard and Ruth Comfort Mitchell are just a few of the San Franciscans who have stood in Montalvo's natural amphitheatre and read their own poetry by "terraced lawns, new mown" near "fountains, whence doves have dipped and flown."

These rococo lines, which seem too high-flown for almost anywhere else, are appropriate to Montalvo, home of the late Senator James Duval Phelan, one-time Mayor of San Francisco.

Phelan gave his faith in the arts more than lip service. On his death in 1930 he bequeathed Montalvo as a "cultural center, to be maintained as a public park . . . under reasonable restrictions . . . and for the development of Art, Literature, Music and Architecture by promising students."

Today the Montalvo Association, and the Santa Clara County Parks and Recreation Department carry on as Phelan would have wished. Writers, composers and painters live and work on the grounds of Montalvo. Art classes and exhibitions are held in the fine old mansion. The carriage house has become a theater.

An arboretum adjoins the garden. An annual music festival encouraged by Yehudi Menuhin brightens the summer season. Although the original acreage has suffered attrition over the years, Phelan's many sets of griffins still guard the entrance and the statuary he celebrated in sonnets stands sightless surrounded by roses.

If the name, Montalvo, seems to ring a distant association bell, go around to the fountain in the court behind the mansion, where a tablet explains that Garcia Ordonez de Montalvo, a Spanish novelist of the 16th century, was first to use the word "California" in print. It appears in *Las Sergas de Esplandian* and describes the area as an island, fabulously rich with gold, inhabited by black Amazons whose queen rode griffins, which also guarded her treasures.

The sour note in Montalvo's idyll was a long court wrangle, now happily resolved. The San Francisco Art Institute, original heirs to the estate, are pleased to be free of the burdens of absentee landlordism, and Montalvo, little changed from Phelan's ideal, has an ending to its saga appropriate to romance.

Sculpture is typical of the romantic flavor of the villa.

41

Palo Alto takes its name from a tree, the tall stake sited by Portola and his men in the plain of white oaks. Later trees give the town a comfortable grace.

The Town that Loves Trees

■ In November of 1769, Don Gaspar de Portola and his men camped for six days by a redwood tree in the great *Llano de los Robles del Puerto de San Francisco*—the Plain of the White Oaks of the Port of San Francisco—better known today as the Santa Clara Valley.

They called their twin-trunked landmark on San Francisquito Creek, *El Palo Alto*, the "tall stake." Subsequent Spanish trail-breakers Anza, Font and Crespi, pioneer journalist Bayard Taylor, the Frenchman Peter Coutts-Paulin Caperon, Senator Leland Stanford, railroad builders and thousands of Stanford University students who came in their wake, easily spotted the tree sticking up over the valley oaks.

The tall stake is still there. No longer isolated. Scraggly. Reduced by one trunk that was swept away in a storm of 1886. Outliving the dominance of the railroad, once despised as desecration, whose nearby bridge and tracks are now considered picturesque. It is barely a landmark amid a sprawl of buildings in the valley it once dominated. Nevertheless, it is significantly there.

For Palo Alto, the town whose name comes from the great old sentinel that has seen all of the Bay Area's recorded history, loves trees.

It considers trees its symbol, calls itself, with reason, "a veritable arboretum," makes roads and sidewalks detour around its trees, grants building variances to protect them, sends tank trucks out to water them, has tree surgeons on call for emergencies, and has a "tree walk," one block south of University Avenue, its main street.

The ideal way to launch this walk is with a stop at the Chamber of Commerce, 725 University Avenue, Palo Alto. For sale here for $1 is a tasteful little book called simply *Trees of Palo Alto*. In it, in addition to some good material about trees that do well in the Bay Area (and advice on how to make them do even better), a walker will find a map that lists and locates the parks of Palo Alto. The tree walk, called the Hamilton Avenue Tree Tour, which includes about 60 trees, is on page 29.

With or without the booklet, the stroll along Hamilton is pleasant indeed. It is that idyllic small-town picture-postcard avenue out of memory where you walked as a child. Behind wide lawns, the houses have porches and the porches have swings.

The trees come fully equipped with blossoms, moonlight on cue, and birds that sing for young lovers.

In the classic tradition, begin this walk at the Post Office. Where else? Hamilton begins at Alma five blocks west. (For historians who would like to seek out *El Palo Alto*, it is also on Alma, at Palo Alto Avenue five blocks north). Once much of downtown Palo Alto had neo-Spanish California Mission architecture, usually white with red tiled roof.

An evergreen pear tree is the one to look for by the Post Office and on the Waverly side, a specimen of the dawn redwood, a cousin of the coastal redwood, first discovered living in China in 1946.

Walk east to find by All Saints Episcopal Church a sugar-plum tree, Irish yew, and a bottlebrush. At the nearby First Methodist Church, the remarkably shaped roof with its inset stained glass windows easily upstages the new young trees here. Continue east to see at 855 Hamilton a fern pine, a Chinese photinia, a golden chain tree and a pepper tree. At 865, a bunya bunya and an Australian bush cherry.

Old timers, like the monkey puzzle tree at 909 Hamilton and the holly at 900, intersperse the rarer types.

The walker who continues, handbook open, can soon

identify a silver wattle, a corkscrew willow, tamarisk, silk oak, karo, boxleaf azara, the golden rain and the maidenhair trees.

You may want to detour to the right on Center Drive to see the eucalyptus in Eleanor Park, a few blocks away.

The great glossy-leaved magnolias are the common street tree of Palo Alto. Flower arrangers covet their unusual seed pods in fall. When you've walked on Hamilton as far as Newell, which intersects Hamilton with an offset, cross the street and walk back on the other side.

By then, you may come to feel, as the people of Palo Alto do, that these beautiful trees are friends.

Palo Alto, the city that loves trees, has a street-tree walk and city trucks to carry and water its treeside "arboretum".

42 *Mission architecture around quadrangles makes Stanford one of the pleasantest campuses in North America.*

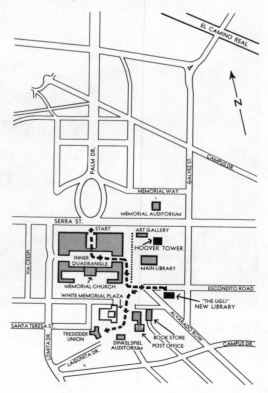

A Walk at Stanford

■ It is sheer size that overwhelms the first-time visitor to "The Farm" as students still call the 8800-acre campus created by Governor and Mrs. Leland Stanford on their Palo Alto stock farm.

"The children of California shall be our children," are the now-famous words the Governor said to his wife in 1884 to assuage her grief not long after the death of their only son, 15-year-old Leland Jr. Stanford University was their way of realizing this lofty resolution. Nowhere else in the world is there a single contiguous private university campus as extensive.

Of this vast acreage, about 5000 is "the heartland" or academic plant, one of the few great university complexes in our country. It lies 31 miles south of San Francisco divided from the city of Palo Alto by El Camino Real. It is too widespread for anyone but hobbits to walk in one day.

There are many beguiling walks and easily five outstanding ones on the Stanford campus. One of the most pleasant is Palm Drive, the long double lane of palms, a campus signature, that leads from downtown Palo Alto's University Avenue to the university's front gate on Serra Street. The walker who arrives by train, as railroad magnate Stanford planned, may want to make his introduction to the campus with this walk.

For openers, those who come by car should begin instead at Serra and Palm Drive, the base of an ovate boulevard, where there is parking, and explore the quadrangle designed by Frederick Law Olmsted.

Take the lay of the land by the Sermon on the Mount mosaic, which looms higher than the other beautifully organized red tile roofs. It is on the face of the Memorial Church facing the Inner Quad.

The other easy landmark is Hoover Tower, named for Herbert Hoover, 31st President of the United States and a member of Stanford's first graduating class.

It was designed by Bakewell and Brown in 1941 and stands southeast of the Inner Quad.

Walk toward the two small towers that mark the entrance to the outer quadrangle, once the site of an elaborate arch ornamented by St. Gaudens. The arch toppled in the 1906 earthquake.

The Stanford Guide Service Information Center, open from 10 a.m. until 5 p.m. daily, is located in the south tower. To identify campus buildings, pick up a map here. Regular tours of the campus are held daily at 2 p.m. from this point. (Groups of more than five should make special arrangements in advance with the Office of University Relations, phone 321-2300, extension 2862.)

Map in hand, to reach the historic core of the campus quickly, walk toward the three arches in the warm yellow sandstone building in front of "memchu" as students nickname the church. Once through it, you are in the Inner Quad.

Notice the roofed arcades, which shelter Stanford students from winter rains and summer heat. Then go into the church to see Roselli's copy of *The Last Supper*. Mrs. Stanford personally obtained papal permission to have this copy made at the Sistine Chapel. If a service is in progress, you are welcome to attend. The church is nonsectarian.

As you step out again, notice the bronze numbers underfoot—class memorial markers. Then go through the left or west gate to reach an extension of Lasuen Street which is reserved for walkers and bicycles. Bear right, away from Hoover Tower, to reach the $5.2 million J. Henry Meyer Memorial

Undergraduate Library, dedicated in December, 1966.

As handsome as this John Carl Warnecke-designed building is, students have nicknamed it "The Ugli," not for its appearance, but in abbreviation of Undergraduate Library. This is typical of Stanford slang in which Hoover Tower becomes "hootow," "flomo' 'is Florence Moore Dormitory, and the White Memorial Plaza nearby is the "mempla."

After exploring the "ugli," head for "mempla" to find a bookstore and Post Office designed by Warnecke and considered to be the most beautiful and functional in the Bay Area. If an absent-minded professor is standing in front of the P.O. boxes, trying to remember his number or name, it might be the much-loved classics scholar, Brooks Otis. Aristedes Demetrios designed the fountain sculpture.

Go up the stairs and bear right at the end of the plaza to reach Tresidder Memorial Union, community center for the 11,000 students. Visitors are welcome at the cafeteria to linger over coffee at the outdoor tables.

To end this walk with a flourish, return to "hootow" and go to the top for an overview of the campus.

43

Half Moon Bay, a village down the coast, has this unusual brown and white Victorian church in its old Spanish Town section. Part of the school adjoining it was once a station for the Ocean Shore railroad.

Village Down the Coast

■ If that great autumnal urge for "Over the river and through the woods to grandfather's house we go" has loomed unsatisfied on your weekends, consider a walk in Spanishtown, one of the most pleasant anachronisms still extant in the Bay Area. It has all the delicious small town flavor, the easy pace, the unspoiled creek banks and little bridges, the general stores, the picket fences, vegetable gardens and grace the pushy tracts have lost.

Spanishtown, which may well be the oldest community in San Mateo County, began when two neighboring rancho owners, Candelario Miramontes and Tiburcio Vasquez, built their homes near the creek that was their joint property line. Authorities differ on the date of the village, but its first cemetery had the years 1820-1923 on its gate and many of the headstones commemorate pioneers born in Spain.

The village life really began when San Benito, as it was first known, became a refuge for unhappy Spanish and Mexican families who fled San Francisco in 1846 "when the Gringo came." Today Spanishtown is the oldest part of Half Moon Bay, 25 miles south of San Francisco on State Highway 1, or the Cabrillo Highway, as this stretch is known. To make this walk turn east off Highway 1 on Kelly Street and park near Index Corner, where Kelly crosses Main.

Pause at the outset to get your bearings. Kelly runs east to the brook called Arroyo Leon and west to the Pacific Ocean at Kelly Beach, a park that is one of the ten beautiful San Mateo State-owned beaches and well provided with picnic tables. Main street runs roughly north and south in the heart of Spanishtown. The name Index Corner came at a time when Half Moon Bay's own telephone company was housed in what now is Cunha's Grocery Store. Here on the coastside, incidentally, one must buy the telephone directory, which is published at $1 to raise funds for Boy Scouts and the school band.

Walk south on Main, noticing the hitching post in front of George's Toggery. When this was the Bortano Saloon, such posts lined all of Main Street. Bear left, or east, on Miramontes Street to reach the unusual brown and white Victorian Gothic Community Methodist Church, built in 1872. According to *Here Today*, the Junior League historic sites book, a wing of the church was once an Ocean Shore Railroad station.

The interesting little building across from it with the sign saying Et Cetera, was built as the office of a country doctor. It also has an office of an attorney who comes one day a week. Walk east to find at 508 San Benito Street a home built in 1870 by a blacksmith named Peter P. Qunlan. Then for fun, go out on the little bridge over Arroyo Leon and linger there awhile, enjoying the gurgle of water over stones, the rustle of leaves on the trees by the bank and possibly bird song. The cemetery visible uphill is recent.

Double back to San Benito and head north on San Benito to Kelly where corn and purple cabbage grow in the yard, a clothesline hangs near the barn and a funky fence encloses the home built by August Bailey, who owned a general store and bakery. Turn west on Kelly to number 751, where a double scallop of shingles borders the roof of Fred Simmons' house, built 106 years ago by his father, Adam, a pioneer undertaker.

At Johnston Street, named for James Johnston, an Ohioan who brought the first wagon down the coast and later subdivided Spanishtown south of Pilarcitos Creek, bear right to 423, the home of Robert Knapp, inventor of the side hill plow.

Continue on Mills to Main Street to find the O'Domenic Hotel, one of the few saloons surviving out of 11 that once served Half Moon Bay. Come south along Main, noticing the general stores and the five and dime. Local announcements, some in Portuguese, grace store windows. Like other coastal communities, Half Moon Bay celebrates the Portuguese Chamarita Festival with processions and feasting in the springtime.

If you're winded, end your walk here where it started. But if the charm of the little village leaves you eager for more, walk two blocks west on Kelly to find at Church Street Our Lady of the Pillar Catholic church, whose bronze bell tolled for the first time in 1868 at an earlier church, since burned, is located in the earliest Pilarcitos cemetery. Then go south, passing the Cunha School, to Miramontes, then east on Miramontes to Purissima where number 546 is a distinguished little pea-green house whose shingled cornice seems to be Christmas lighted all year. End your day's excursion on the beach to find the great attraction for the old Californios, as well as the newer ones in Spanishtown.

Half Moon Bay Beach is usually foggy in the summer but sunny in the winter.

Index